To Ina,

With our love & best wishes.

Margaret & Tom.

Thank you for visiting us, we have enjoyed every minute of your stay. Wish it could have been longer. M.

Beautiful
New Zealand

Beautiful
New Zealand

Errol Brathwaite

Published by David Bateman
Distributed by Gordon and Gotch

Contents

Prepared by Deans International Publishing
52–54 Southwark Street, London SE1 1UA
A division of The Hamlyn Publishing Group Limited
London · New York · Sydney · Toronto

First published in New Zealand by
David Bateman Ltd.
30/34 View Road, Glenfield, Auckland 10

Distributed in New Zealand by
Gordon and Gotch Ltd.
2 Carr Road, Mt. Roskill, Auckland 4

Copyright © The Hamlyn Publishing Group Limited 1985
ISBN 0-908610-27-0

Printed in Singapore

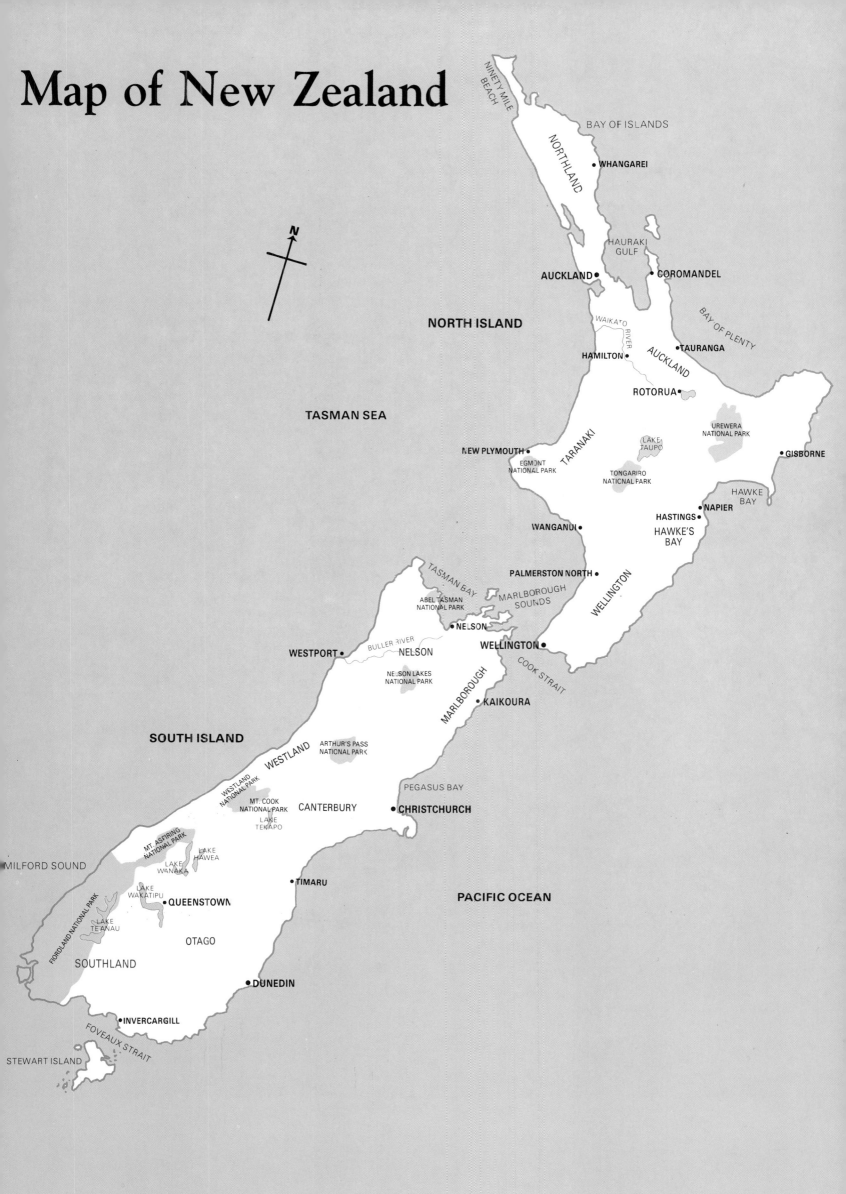

Map of New Zealand

NINETY MILE BEACH

BAY OF ISLANDS

NORTHLAND

• WHANGAREI

HAURAKI GULF

AUCKLAND •
• COROMANDEL

NORTH ISLAND

WAIKATO RIVER

BAY OF PLENTY

AUCKLAND

• TAURANGA

HAMILTON •

ROTORUA •

UREWERA NATIONAL PARK

TASMAN SEA

NEW PLYMOUTH •

TARANAKI

LAKE TAUPO

• GISBORNE

EGMONT NATIONAL PARK

TONGARIRO NATIONAL PARK

HAWKE BAY

HASTINGS • NAPIER

WANGANUI •

HAWKE'S BAY

PALMERSTON NORTH •

WELLINGTON

TASMAN BAY

MARLBOROUGH SOUNDS

ABEL TASMAN NATIONAL PARK

• NELSON

WESTPORT •

BULLER RIVER

NELSON

WELLINGTON •

COOK STRAIT

NELSON LAKES NATIONAL PARK

MARLBOROUGH

• KAIKOURA

SOUTH ISLAND

WESTLAND

ARTHUR'S PASS NATIONAL PARK

WESTLAND NATIONAL PARK

PEGASUS BAY

MT. COOK NATIONAL PARK

CANTERBURY

• CHRISTCHURCH

LAKE TEKAPO

MT. ASPIRING NATIONAL PARK

LAKE HAWEA

MILFORD SOUND

LAKE WANAKA

• TIMARU

PACIFIC OCEAN

LAKE WAKATIPU

• QUEENSTOWN

FIORDLAND NATIONAL PARK

LAKE TE ANAU

OTAGO

SOUTHLAND

• DUNEDIN

• INVERCARGILL

FOVEAUX STRAIT

STEWART ISLAND

A view from the Port Hills of Lyttelton, the port for Christchurch, sheltering in Lyttelton Harbour on Banks Peninsula

Introduction

Poplars and a farm-shed in hills near Queenstown – an unexpectedly gentle
scene amid the rugged mountains of north-west Otago

A romantically minded Englishman who came to New Zealand last
century expecting to find a cluster of tropical islands, and found a
landscape on a vaster scale than that from which he had come, bemusedly
called it "a quart in a pint pot". It just couldn't be that big! But it was.

The country still takes first-time visitors in just that way.

The fact is that New Zealand is a land of engaging contradictions, and
that always takes people by surprise. Regarded by the world (and often,
indeed, by its own inhabitants), as small to insignificant, it is actually
about a quarter as large again as mainland Britain. Where, however, the
British Isles are home to a population of around fifty-six million people,
New Zealand is inhabited by slightly less than three and a half million,
who even so exhibit an astonishing range of regional characteristics.

Predominantly Anglo-Saxon in outlook, the population of New Zealand nevertheless describes itself variously as South-East Asian, Australa-
sian, Polynesian, or, diminishingly, British. Individually, however, New
Zealanders think of themselves as English, Irish, Scottish, Dutch, Yugoslav, Chinese, Maori or Samoan, to say nothing of a respectable number
of more recently arrived ethnic minorities who think of themselves
determinedly as Kiwi.

From New Zealand has come a surprising company of statesmen,
soldiers, sailors, airmen, scientists, athletes, singers, actors, writers and
agriculturalists who have stood tall on the world's stage. It was New
Zealand that led the western world into the era of the Welfare State, and
was for many years regarded as the social laboratory of the world. It was a
New Zealander who built, if not the world's first aeroplane, then at least

Christ's College, one of several boys' private schools in Christchurch, was
planned by the city's Anglican founders

the very first such machine to incorporate such "modern" features as
variable-pitch propeller, ailerons, trimming control and steerable nose-
wheel – at about the same time as the Wright Brothers were shakily
staggering into the air with their first successful and infinitely cruder
machine. It was a New Zealander who invented and produced the world's
first marine jet engine. And, on the subject of matters maritime, a New
Zealander was, quite recently, Britain's First Sea Lord.

It was a New Zealander who first split the atom.

Eminently, delightfully inhabitable, with a temperate to sub-tropical
climate range, New Zealand is also geographically full of surprises. Within
its 270,000 square kilometres (103,000-odd square miles), it is a vast and
generous sampling of practically every type of terrain, every kind of
environment, that the rest of the globe can show – a swatch-book, if you
like, of samples of almost all that the world has to offer.

"A land rising high," Captain James Cook called it, gazing at it in
some awe from the quarterdeck of his cockle-shell ex-collier in the late
eighteenth century; and well he might, for so it is, especially along almost
the whole length of the South Island's west coast, where the Southern
Alps rear up almost from the sea's edge to dazzling, snow-clad peaks, over
two hundred of them more than 2286m (7500ft) high. thirty-five of them
higher than 2743m (9000ft), a select and breathtaking group in the
central massif towering higher than 3352m (11,000ft), clustered about the
awesome Mount Cook, (Aorangi, "The Cloud Piercer"), 3764m
(12,349ft) in altitude.

"Ao-tea-roa! Land of the Long White Cloud!" exclaimed the early

Lake Matheson, nestling under an ancient moraine of Westland's Fox Glacier, is famous for its mirror images of the Southern Alps

Maori voyagers, for that is how the east coast of the northern North Island appeared to them, with its low-lying coastline, its deeply indented bays and long, winding, mangrove-choked harbours and waterways, sometimes shrouded in smoke and steam from prodigious thermal activity.

Between those geographical and scenic extremes is a wealth of forests of sub-tropical luxuriance, into some of which descend mighty glaciers from eternal snowfields; immense patchworks of plains dotted with villages and market towns, traversed by rivers which are tangled skeins of gravel-choked waterways, and geometrically divided by networks of long, arrow-straight roads; rolling, limestone-ribbed hills of pleasant green, and pretty pastoral dales; cities that might have been transplanted *in toto* from England or Scotland, yet have since acquired a flavour of their own; country hamlets with friendly pubs that have more than a touch of the Irish about them; trout streams open to anyone with a couple of dollars for a licence. There are, too, purely antipodean cities in tapestries of forested hills around landlocked harbours in which, as was said of one of them, "half the world's navies might ride in perfect security".

In the sub-alpine highlands are lakes like captive seas, of unimaginable depth. On a high North Island plateau, and dotted here and there down the length of both islands, thermal areas quake and steam. There are active volcanoes – on which people ski; and there are deserts of shifting sand dunes, or of pumice clothed with unique plant life. Along the coastlines are golden-sand beaches stretching uninhabited, or dotted with holiday settlements, for thirty-odd kilometres (18¾ miles) in an unbroken sweep; and deep fiords whose walls rise sheer to heights of up to 1524m (5000ft).

A world-famous image of New Zealand: a hot spring erupts into a geyser of boiling steam and water at Rotorua, on the North Island's thermal plateau

The superb sands of Matapouri beach are just a short drive from Whangarei, the only city and main port of Northland

New Zealand is rugged – and gentle; noisily crowded – and silently empty; prettily tended and groomed by patient husbandry – or cheerfully unkempt where huge flocks of sheep graze; warm enough to grow tropical fruit – and sub-antarctic enough to be home to whales, seals and penguins: an engaging pot pourri of snow and sunshine, surf and willow-shaded streams, forest and field, big-city stridency and rural peace.

It is pointless to come looking for architectural consequence, though there are interesting and historic buildings to see. New Zealand's fascination lies mainly in two things, scenic splendour and people – and even the people have been largely shaped and subtly changed by the land, so that the Polynesians are no longer quite so Polynesian as the Polynesian Polynesians – so to speak – and the English are English with a difference, and Scots have almost lost the burr of highlands or lowlands from their speech after one or two New Zealand-born generations, but are still Caledonian in outlook and temperament, and Irish retain an Irish lyricism in their conversation and their writing though the brogue died a couple of generations ago.

In both land and people there is this rich variety within the compass of 2–3,000 easy road-kilometres (1200–1900 miles), and the average distance between places of particular scenic, historical or general "tourist" interest would be in the order of 50–100 kilometres (31–62 miles); a whole world in this remarkably compact, singularly beautiful package.

The ancient Polynesians who came to it from comparatively tiny dots of land across the Pacific, overwhelmed at its generous proportions and unfailing bounty, might well have breathed their prayer to Rehua, the god of kindness: "Tena te mana o Rehua! Behold the greatness of Rehua!"

Which, when you come to think about it, is just another way of marvelling at "a quart in a pint pot".

Behold, then, Rehua's greatness.

The traditional songs, chants and dances of the Maori people retain an
important place in their culture today

Pleasure craft at anchor in the Bay of Islands, where 150 islands are dotted over the waters of the bay, which is famous for its big-game fishing

Northland

Orewa, the "Hibiscus Coast" resort, spreads along this magnificent sandy beach

To the north of the city of Auckland lies the long Northland peninsula, in shape not unlike the *maripi*, the serrated, convex-edged knife of the Maori. It is probably true to say of it that most New Zealanders, from Auckland southward, have a vague mental picture of Northland as being a thin stick of land, a mere appendage, pointing roughly northward. They would concede, if pressed, that it is embellished somewhere along its jagged eastern edge by the magnificent Bay of Islands, and that it possesses one small city, Whangarei, somewhere about the middle.

The reason for this vagueness probably lies in the fact that Northland, within still vigorous living memory, used to be one of three isolated areas of New Zealand, at least to the extent that getting into them required nerves of steel and a robust constitution. It isn't true now, of course, of any of them. Northland has long had excellent road, rail and air links with the rest of the country, and travel is easy and pleasant – and, to those same New Zealanders, pleasantly surprising.

For Northland, when you motor through it, turns out to be unexpectedly capacious. It makes up, after all, slightly more than a third of the length of the North Island. The distance, as the crow flies, from Auckland to North Cape is about the same as the distance from London to Manchester. The width of the peninsula at its widest point is more than 80 kilometres (50 miles). And within that area, it contains an amount and variety of scenery finer, perhaps, than any comparable area in the rest of the North Island.

Historically, it is the birthplace of the nation, a threshold country

Ponga, one of the characteristic ferns of New Zealand's luxuriant bush areas

where both Maori and European settlement had its beginnings. Events that occurred there have had a tremendous influence on the shape and style of New Zealand life, and the aftermath of those events is still being felt politically today.

Northland was the first choice of habitation for the very good reason that its climate is on the warm side of temperate, bordering on the sub-tropical. Its soil is largely volcanic, with the added advantage of vast reefs of limestone in its framework. It possesses many fine harbours, and is well watered, with one or two rivers navigable for small ships such as the scows and coastal schooners and canoes that formed the bulk of the pioneers' transport and communications. It was also covered with what must have seemed to the pioneers to be an infinite supply of excellent timber.

Historically and geographically, Northland may be roughly divided into three major regions. To the south there once spread great *kauri* forests, which were greedily felled and milled for their superb timber. On this region's west coast stretches the landlocked 65-kilometre (40-mile) expanse of Kaipara Harbour, comparatively shallow, yet quite deep enough for the scows and schooners which sailed easily up the harbour's branches, into the heart of the forests. The forests themselves grew right down to the water's edge, and Kaipara Harbour must have seemed ready-made for the establishing of milling communities.

On the east coast, where the spurs of the ranges come down to dip their points into the sea, the beaches and coves are pleasant inlets, guarded by high, forest-crowned promontories. Here, too, there was

Colonial elegance preserved in the Puhoi hotel, which contains relics from the time when the tiny settlement was founded by Bohemians from Staab

timber for the taking, and sheltered havens in which to load and carry it off for the building of a hundred fast-growing towns and settlements.

Northward from Cape Rodney on the east coast, the coastline swings in two 20-kilometre (12-mile) bights separated by a headland known as Bream Tail, to Whangarei Harbour. From there, the coast forms that convex-edged, serrated *maripi*-blade curve, rich in delightful seascapes and safe harbours, deep coves and long, serpentine inlets, centred upon the magnificent Bay of Islands, and terminating in a glorious sweep of uninterrupted beach around Doubtless Bay, where the *maripi* handle joins the blade. In this region are the remaining *kauri* forests and, on the west coast and reaching some 33 kilometres (20-odd miles) almost to the centre-line of the peninsula, is the twisting, many-branched Hokianga Harbour. All of this is real "threshold" country, site of early missionary activity, a smiling land with rich soil and a coast teeming with fish.

The third region is the handle of the *maripi*, the stick of high land 5 kilometres (3 miles) wide at its narrowest point, 12 kilometres (7½ miles) at its widest, if you don't count the "pommel" at the top of the handle. A strange region, with its long sweeps of beach and its high, windswept lonelinesses, it is one of the richest of all the districts in Maori lore.

There are two main routes northward out of Auckland. There is the Western Motorway, which skirts the western arm of Waitemata Harbour, and there is the route which crosses the Auckland Harbour Bridge and runs through the north-eastern suburbs to rejoin Route One at Albany. The western route is perhaps the more interesting of the two, winding gently through farms and orchards and vineyards – great wine country, this – and from which, at Kumeu, a road branches off to Helensville.

Timber milling first began half way up the peninsula, near Whangarei, but its beginnings as a great industry were here, at Helensville, initiated

Whangarei, here photographed from Parahaki Hill, was settled as early as 1839
and is today the regional centre of Northland

by one John McLeod and his brother, Isaac. John began timber milling and Isaac began farming on the cleared land, supplying food to the timber workers. John and Isaac built substantial homes – of *kauri*, naturally – and John named his after his wife, calling it, simply, Helen's Villa. The name was adopted as the name of the township that grew here, and was soon shortened to Helensville.

Today, with the timber long gone, Helensville is notable, first for its spa – there are hot springs here – and secondly for its cheeses, of the Gouda and Leidenz types.

The countryside is open, rather untidy, with its hummocky pastures and its hedges of *toetoe* (pampas grass), as good dairying country is apt to be. The town is set at the broad end of a long valley which was probably once itself an arm of the Kaipara Harbour. The surrounding landscape is rolling land, slightly higher and steeper to the north-east, heavily patched with scrub and surviving stands of taller timber.

The really spectacular country in this region is concentrated along the east coast, a cross-country drive from Helensville of no great distance through Kaukapakapa and Silverdale to Orewa, where the road keeps company with a fine sweep of golden-sand beach, interrupted along its 10-kilometre (6-mile) length only by the Wainui ("Big Water") river. The inland side of the road is lined with an almost unbroken facade of motels, homes and eating houses.

Waiwera and Puhoi

The scenery changes suddenly and dramatically at the end of Orewa Beach, as the way leaps up and swings around a steep shoulder, densely, darkly, richly forested, the lovely native bush asterisked with the paler green of magnificent tree ferns called *ponga*, but invariably pronounced, for some rule-bending reason, as *punga* (rhymes with hung-a). This is the Waiwera Hill Scenic Reserve, and it is provided with rest areas into which a motorist may turn, park, and sit and enjoy the remarkable vistas of this spectacular coastline.

For spectacular it has now become. To the west, the 3000 kilometres (1875 miles) of fretted coastline of the Kaipara Harbour has a somewhat monotonous sameness along its entire length. Here, in the east, begins a succession of peninsulas, inlets and bays sheltered by islands which stand across their mouths, protected on their flanks by forest-crowned bluffs, their shores almost uniform crescents of smooth sand.

The first of these is Waiwera Beach – the name means "Hot Water" – where the village has grown up about what must be one of the most romantically sited, pleasant spas on earth.

The place is named, obviously, from the hot springs. They issue from the forested hillsides behind the resort hotel, and they well up through the sand of a Treasure-Island beach, whose guardian promontories are covered with olive-green native bush splashed in season with white clematis and yellow *kowhai*, with a fringe of scarlet *pohutukawa*. The place is musical with the chiming song of bellbirds and the virtuosity of song-thrushes, and mysterious at night with the cries of the little owls.

The original spa was built by an enterprising 20-year-old Scotsman named David Graham, who arrived here by horse-drawn buggy and what must have been sheer dogged persistence, since the only roads were the paths trodden hitherto by barefoot Maoris through virgin forest; and at one point he, his horse and his buggy had to be lowered down a cliff-face by manpowered ropes.

A popular picnic spot near Whangarei: the 24-m (80-ft) Whangarei Falls on the Hatea River where it flows through an attractive bush reserve

Captain Cook named Piercy Island, in the Bay of Islands, after a Lord of the Admiralty, Sir Piercy Brett, a jocular reference to the hole piercing the rock

The village which grew up around the spa has now lost most of its Victorian and Edwardian elegance, and the original hotel has also gone; but there are still a couple of old villas, almost gingerbread in appearance, built by Bohemian craftsmen from Puhoi, a few kilometres inland.

Puhoi is in the midst of a countryside different again from this extravagantly beautiful coast. It appears quite suddenly from a point where the road climbs over the crest of a rise, a slightly puzzling vista, being in New Zealand and quite definitely of New Zealand, yet suggesting in some vague particular something which is foreign. The mind plays with a suggestion of Central Europe, in spite of the post-and-wire fences with the lichened, wedge-split battens and rough *totara* posts, the cheerfully scruffy hills patched with dark green forest. For there, on the roadside, stands a wayside Calvary, freshly painted white and blue, with a little offering of fresh flowers before it. And the clutch of typically nineteenth-century New Zealand farmhouses, each with its cluster of outbuildings, do not stand remote from each other in the midst of their acres as New Zealand farmhouses do, but huddle together to form a straggling little village, with the farms radiating around them, in the European pattern.

The first white settlers in this valley were families who came from Staab, then a small village on the outskirts of Prague. The first batch arrived in the midwinter of 1863, on a black night in appalling weather, and immediately with first light, began carving out homes for themselves. They almost starved in the first years, completely isolated from other centres of settlement, both by the ruggedness of the land, and the fact that they spoke no English. They wrote home, cheerful letters telling their friends and relations not to worry about them, that they were prospering. The result was that just when they were beginning at last to feel secure, a second batch arrived from the Fatherland, and the entire settlement was plunged back to near-starvation again.

In the Puhoi pub their relics are to be found, foreign, like the names on the memorial tablets in the village church – Schollum, Schischka, Straker, Bayer. In the pub, too, may sometimes be heard the dudelsack, thoroughgoing Teutonic answer to the bagpipes of Scotland or Ireland, sweeter-toned than either, and elevated, with true German ingenuity, to something of a mechanical marvel.

This southern region of Northland may be conveniently taken to end at Warkworth, which sits prettily on the bush-clad banks of the Mahurangi river estuary, surrounded by farms and orchards in a gentling countryside, though one still bounded by that magnificent coastline of deep bays and tidal creeks that escape into the Hauraki Gulf between jutting headlands of tree-crowned rock. Sitting where it shelters the cove, but some distance out from it, is Kawau Island, with its old elegant Mansion House, one-time residence of Governor Sir George Grey, colonial trouble-shooter, a sort of Victorian Kissinger, who later became Prime Minister of New Zealand. Grey stocked the island with exotic animals, including zebras to pull his carriage, but few of his menagerie survived for very long. One species which did was a type of wallaby from Australia, a type now very rare on that continent. The Mansion House, after serving for a good many years as a guest house, is now a museum. The bay in which it is situated is a favourite resort of yachtsmen. The island is delightful, with its bush and its walks, its secret little coves and its old copper-mine ruins, like a castle on its small promontory.

Waipu and Whangarei

Where the two broad bights begin their northward sweep up to Whangarei, the township of Waipu sits between two tributary streams of the Waipu river, which flows out over a flat, fat plain. The town was built by Scottish immigrants who fled to Nova Scotia after the Sutherland clearances, but who were persuaded – perhaps because they placed the earlier Nova Scotian immigrants in a similar position to the first Bohemians at Puhoi? – to move to Australia. Not liking the Australian climate, they crossed to New Zealand in 1856–59, and on this plain they prospered.

Unlike the Bohemians, they had ready contact with Whangarei, already a thriving settlement.

Whangarei Harbour, like most Northland harbours, is broad and shallow. It has channels for deep-sea vessels, and deep-water berthage. At its mouth, at Marsden Point, it has an oil refinery, where the great ocean-going tankers discharge.

The name, Whangarei, has been translated as "Bountiful Harbour", but a more likely explanation is that it derives from "Whanga-rei-terenga-paraoa", which signifies a haven for leaping, swimming whales.

The Maoris first settled here, choosing the hilly ground at the northern end of the harbour because the harbourside land, being fertile and well-favoured, was much coveted by other tribes, and the occupants needed the hills on which to site their *pas*, a *pa* being a fort or a fortified village. The *Pakeha* (white or European), who came first to trade, naturally settled where the business was – and prospered.

Whangarei looks prosperous. The living was always comparatively easy, the soil rich, producing bumper crops of *kumara* (sweet potato), gourd, and pretty well every kind of fruit and vegetable in the Anglo-Saxon diet. The waters of the harbour have always been rich in shellfish such as mussels, *paua* (abalone), *pipi* (a small clam), rock oysters and scallops. The offshore islands and reefs just outside the harbour abound in crayfish – or did when reasonably conserved.

The strongest *pa* in the vicinity was on Parahaki Hill, 242m (794ft) high, around the foot of which the city wraps itself, and the Hatea river curves like a moat. Of the *pa* there is now no readily visible trace.

Today a pretty, peaceful township in the Bay of Islands, Russell began life as a notorious "hell-hole" of ex-convicts, deserters and whaling crews

Pompallier House, a *pisé-de-terre* building where Bishop Pompallier printed his Gospels, dates from the 1870s

Parahaki, named in honour of a valiant, forlorn-hope action by its defenders when its fall was imminent, is now a bush reserve. The hill is surmounted by a tall obelisk of stainless steel faced with an illuminated Cross and topped by a perpetually burning lamp, a monument to the dead of two World Wars, and sundry lesser conflicts in which New Zealanders have taken part.

From Parahaki's summit, a panoramic view may be obtained of the city, which from this viewpoint doesn't seem to be large enough to be called a city at all. Officially it is, since Whangarei, while making no claim to a place amongst the world's great cities, was nevertheless accorded the dignity of cityhood in 1964. So at least it's one of the world's newest.

In any case, it cannot all be seen from even this high grandstand; for Whangarei is closely woven into the fabric of the forest which makes up the greater part of all that you can see. There are numerous bush reserves, all within minutes of the main street, so that from the roar of traffic and the clatter of typewriters, a five-minute walk takes city workers into their choice of cool, bird-haunted glades from which the traffic noise can hardly be heard, and all is peace and filtered green light.

Whangarei began life as a sawmilling centre, and first became wealthy on *kauri* gum, fossilised sap from prehistoric *kauri* forests, as other towns became wealthy on gold. The gum used to be highly sought after for the manufacture of superior paints and varnishes.

From Whangarei came the first Maori ever to visit England. His name was Mahanga, a simple, forthright man who enjoyed himself immensely in London, where he met the Royal Family. George III disappointed him, being no great warrior as Mahanga had expected, but a frail old man who "could neither throw a spear nor fire a musket". Mahanga reported that Queen Charlotte was kind, "putting her hand under her mat, into a little

26

The Church of St Paul, Paihia, the fourth on the site, was built in 1925 as a memorial to the brother missionaries, the Rev. Henry and the Rev. William Williams

bag that was there, and took out of it some red money – guineas – and gave it to me", and he "got myself a wife with some of Queen Charlotte's money. Her name was Nancy. She was very fond of me, and proved pregnant. She used to ask me if the child, when born, would go to New Zealand, and if it would have marks on its face like the *moko* (tattoo) on mine." Alas, poor Mahanga, on his return, told of the wonders he had seen, and promptly got himself the reputation among his own people of being something of a Maori Munchausen.

There is practically every type of natural beauty in the vicinity. There are lofty, still slightly jagged peaks, forged in the fires of ancient volcanoes, still being tamed and rounded by wind and rain, still interestingly shaped, feeding the imagination and stimulating the inventive mind. It is easy to understand why Maori lore in this region is so rich in legend, myth and fairy tale.

One great bluff, overlooking McLeod's Bay on the northern shores of the harbour, is topped by formations of basalt which are said to be the figures of Manaia, a local chief, Hautatu, his fighting chief, and Hautatu's wife, Pito, plus two illegitimate children fathered by Manaia after sending Hautatu far away to do battle. The tale is not unlike the biblical story of David and Bathsheba, except that in this instance, the wronged husband survived the war and came back, and was pursuing Manaia and Pito and the children, when the old gods turned them all into stone.

Just to the north of Whangarei, on the city's outskirts, is Kamo, where another small spa offers beneficial waters, cold this time. Kamo Springs, carbonated chalybeate waters, gush forth from the ground with considerable force, and are organised into baths. Although the water is cold, patients sitting in it experience a curious, comfortable warmth, caused by the close garment of bubbles which form all over the skin, trapping body heat most efficiently.

The Treaty House at Waitangi, built by the British Resident, James Busby, in 1833. The Treaty of Waitangi was signed in front of the house in 1840

Bay of Islands

From the limestone hills and old volcanic cones about Whangarei, the road dips down into shallow, broad valleys and runs between strangely regular hummocks of bush- and scrub-covered hills. About 30 kilometres (19 miles) north of Whangarei, the village of Towai sits on the edge of just such a valley, with its back to a steep series of razorback ridges, which rise up, steep and high, between Towai and the coast. Today largely sheep and cattle pasture, the hills are still partially clad in a remnant of the great jungle through which, in 1845, British forces had to march, manhandling their field guns, to one of the major engagements in the war fought by the Ngapuhi people and the Government. The chief, Kawiti, built a massive *pa* on a sloping face in that tangle of spurs and ridges, from which he could see the arrival and departure of warships and troopships in the Bay of Islands. He built it complete with shellproof

The Maoris' traditional *whare-runanga* is usually symbolic of a tribal ancestor. His head is represented by the *koruru* (mask), his arms by the *maihi* (bargeboards)

shelters (the Maori was a quick learner in matters military), massive palisades, and sufficient thicknesses of flax matting across the faces of the palisading to absorb musket balls. He called his *pa* Ruapekapeka, "The Bat's Cave", and he filled it with warriors armed with shotguns, muskets and long-handled tomahawks, traditional wood and stone weapons, and a 12-pounder carronade. The British artillery made no impression on the *pa*, though a lucky shot hit the carronade in the muzzle, putting it out of action, but that was all.

Eventually, the Maoris, being Christians, were having a Sunday church service at the back of the *pa*, and the soldiers seized that moment to attack. Most of the Maoris got away, leaving Colonel Despard to dismantle the *pa* and return to the Bay of Islands.

Today you can wander over the site, peering into the shellproof *ruas* (storage pits), or you can sit on Kawiti's carronade, the shard of broken muzzle lying beside it still, and you can look out across those heartbreaking ridges to the shining expanse of the Bay of Islands, 30 kilometres distant, looking pretty much as Kawiti saw it from this spot, 140 years ago.

It all happened a very long time ago – yet what is 140 years? About another kilometre along the road from the Ruapekapeka turnoff is another side-road leading down to the Waiomio Caves, owned by the Kawiti family and famous for their glow-worm displays.

Paihia and Russell

The township of Paihia, on the shores of the Bay of Islands, lies about 20 kilometres (12 miles) north of the village of Kawakawa, from which Colonel Despard's force started that frightful grind inland through virgin forest and over those nightmare ridges to Ruapekapeka. Paihia was originally a mission station, wherein laboured Church of England men who, in another age and faith, might well have been canonised. At the end of a long sweep of beach where the Bay of Islands' tides lap gently at Paihia's toes, and across the narrow estuary of the Waitangi river, safest of anchorages for pleasure craft, is the rise of green headland on which still stands the house from which colonial New Zealand was originally governed. The official British Residency gazes blankly across the bay at once rowdy, unofficial Kororareka, the "Hell-hole of the Pacific", now peaceful

Rocks and islets dot the turquoise-blue water around Kerikeri inlet in the Bay of Islands

---

Russell, which clusters, as did Kororareka before it, above a strip of gravel beach which, sheltered by a high headland, is as safe an anchorage for a flotilla of pleasure craft as it was for whalers and trading schooners in the 1840s. Perhaps today the town ventures a little higher up the saddle which stretches between Flagstaff Hill and the bush-covered peak over-looking Matauwhi Bay than it did in the '40s of last century, but it is, nevertheless, not difficult to picture the old town of Kororareka. There are still quaint (but comfortable) hotels and shops. The house of Bishop Pompallier, the Catholic missionary-bishop – which is now said by the Historic Places Trust not to have been his dwelling at all, but to have housed his printing press – still dreams in its sub-tropical garden. The little white wooden Christ Church still stands watch over its brood of gravestones. There is still – or, perhaps it would be better to say, again – a flagstaff on Flagstaff Hill, at the northern end of the town.

But it is not, for all that, the same town. In the war of 1845, between Hone Heke and Kawiti and their Ngapuhi warriors, and the British, Hone Heke's men captured the small blockhouse and chopped down the flagpole by way of opening hostilities. (They had already chopped down the flagpole several times before.) When a handful of bluejackets and marines fought a desperate hand-to-hand donnybrook around Christ Church in the grey light of early morning, they were just forty-five strong against a yelling, berserk, howling mob of about two hundred Maoris. Even so, these marines and sailors from HMS *Hazard* charged, bayonet and cutlass against long-handled tomahawk, *tupara* ("two barrel"; the double-barrelled shotgun, favourite weapon of the Maoris), and cut their way into their midst. Not much weight was added to their charge by the one shot they managed to get off at the Ngapuhi from their one cannon. A cannon ball does not do too much damage to two hundred men in wide open formation. Still, the noise of it dented Maori morale a little. The 'Hazards' chased the Maoris into the scrub; but it couldn't last, with the odds so overwhelmingly in Maori favour, and British determination was set at nought when a civilian, working in the town's powder magazine with a lighted pipe in his mouth, dropped a spark. Up went the magazine, down went British hopes of saving the town, and Kororareka was evacuated, with the chivalrous Ngapuhi not merely allowing civilians and troops to go unmolested, but actually helping to ferry them out to ships in the bay – even while fighting was still going on in the town. Then they looted, pillaged, got drunk on captured grog and burnt the town to the ground, scrupulously sparing Christ Church, Bishop Pompallier's house and all mission buildings.

Christ Church still bears the scars of this encounter, and the Royal Navy still undertakes the task of maintaining the grave of the 'Hazard' men who were killed there.

Pleasantly sited at the foot of the hill which marks the town's boundary is Pompallier House. Bishop Pompallier was a French Roman Catholic missionary, who bought the land on which the house stands, together with a cottage already on the site, from a man named Benjamin Turner, a grog seller and consequently a man of comparative wealth and influence in this raucous town. Turner sold the land on 6 July 1839 to the Bishop, who paid him £370 for it, a grossly inflated price, since Turner had bought it a year earlier for £45.

The remains of Father Peter Chanel, who was murdered at his mission on the island of Futuna in the Wallis Islands group, just north of Fiji, were kept at Pompallier House between 1842 and 1849, when they were taken home to France. In 1954 he was canonised St Peter Chanel, and his shrine, standing quite close to the Anglican Christ Church, is the only place of Christian pilgrimage in Australasia, some say in the southern hemisphere.

All the while that Russell/Kororareka was a roaring, grog-swilling sink of iniquity, Paihia, on the opposite, mainland shore was staidly, virtuously industrious, being a mission station and therefore a hive of decent toil. As with Russell/Kororareka, there is little left of the original Paihia; not because it received the Sodom-and-Gomorrah treatment of Kororareka, but simply because it has changed in the course of time. Not that it is big even now; but there are some fine houses, and a lovely church which Archdeacon Williams, founder of the mission, and in whose memory it was built, never saw.

He would have been hard put to it to have found a better place for his mission. The Maoris were a friendly, generous lot, belonging to the powerful Ngapuhi tribe, locally headed by Hone Heke, nephew of the infamous Hongi Ika of Kerikeri, farther up the coast. They lived in a locality where the climate was kind, the forests rich in bird life, the seas generous and the soil productive. They feared nothing and envied none. They welcomed the ex-naval officer, Williams, and he, for his part, was the kind of bluff, transparently honest, naturally courteous man who gets on well with anyone. They even gave him a nickname, Karuwha, "Four-Eyes", because of the spectacles he wore. He won their love and respect to such a degree that he was able to move freely amongst them even when they were at war with the British.

The locality was ideal in other ways. The land slopes up from the bay, the high and forested hills at the settlement's back sheltering it, tilting it towards the sun. There was timber for ship-building, and a gently shelving beach for ship-launching, and here Williams built and launched his mission ship, *Herald*, in 1826, on a spot now marked by a bronze plaque.

Another bronze plaque marks the spot where, in 1834, a young Welshman named William Colenso set up and operated New Zealand's first printing press.

Today, Paihia stretches along a frontage which extends almost the full length of two bays, Paihia Bay and Horotutu Bay. As bays go, these are pretty shallow indentations, and would be a single sweep of white sand but for the rocky promontory called, with apparently singular unoriginality, Flagstaff Hill. The name, however, is not the product of mental laziness. This little headland, with its cloak of *pohutukawa* draped carelessly about its shoulder, was, literally, a flagstaff hill, the eminence upon which the mast of a shipping signal station was erected. The hill of the same name and tragic memory at Russell served the same purpose. There are probably a hundred flagstaff hills along this coast.

From Paihia, the big-game fishing launches go out into the bay, whose islands range in size from rough-hewn, craggy rocks like the Black Rocks, like shaggy, Rodin-esque statues on flat plinths, to larger islands such as Roberton Island, as it is called in some tourist brochures, though its name on many maps is Motuarohia, (the "Reconnoitred Island"), with its exquisite twin lagoons, near which Captain Cook anchored in 1769; and Urupukapuka Island – in English, "The Island Where Stands the Grove of Broadleaf Trees", site of novelist Zane Grey's beloved fishing camp, Otehei Bay Lodge.

Launch sightseeing trips operate over these waters, the most spectacular being the Cape Brett Cruise via Red Head Passage, around Piercy Island, or Motu Kakaho, the "Island of the Crow", to give it its Maori name, into the Grand Cathedral Cave, and through the famous Hole in the Rock.

Every island has its story, one of the most fascinating concerning Moturua, ("Island of the Cave"), where the French navigator Marion du Fresne landed in 1772 to establish a hospital camp for sick crew members. Unwittingly, the Frenchmen violated some *tapu* – sacred or forbidden thing – on the mainland, and du Fresne and twenty-six of his men were killed and eaten. For anyone interested in a treasure hunt, du Fresne's second-in-command, Crozet, formally took possession of the country for France, and buried documentary evidence in a jar on Moturua. The jar has never been discovered. (It would not make New Zealand French even if it were, since Captain Cook had already annexed New Zealand to Britain.)

Across the Waitangi mouth from Horotutu Bay is the Residency. On the south bank, in 1840, thousands of Maoris from many tribes encamped, a gathering reminiscent of the barons at Runnymede. The simile is apt, for they had gathered to discuss and sign the Treaty of Waitangi, sometimes known as the Maori Magna Carta, a document unique in the annals of colonialism. It was intended to guarantee the Maoris peaceful and undisturbed possession of their lands, to curb land-shark practices by seeing to it that land was bought and sold only by or through the Government, and to offer the signatories the full rights and protection of British citizens.

The Residency, now known as the Treaty House, on whose sloping lawn the signing took place, has seen many gatherings in times of national rejoicing since that day; 6 February 1840, when 512 chiefs, after much discussion, signed the Treaty. The house itself is beautiful, a white wooden house of superb design, appearing deceptively small, yet inside proving astonishingly roomy. The walls are weatherboarded and the roof shingled, and generous French windows with louvred shutters look out on to a simple, ample veranda. Designed by the Colonial Architect in Sydney in the Georgian style of domestic architecture then popular in

Delightful little Kerikeri has a pleasantly cosmopolitan air, a result of its
settlement by people from many European countries

Australia and the United States, but keeping to the simple proportions of
English Georgian, it was built of local materials, and with Australian
jarrah flooring and framing and Australian cedar for the casement doors.
Airy and cool in the summer, yet with no room so large that it cannot be
adequately heated by its simply-designed fireplace, it must have been
extremely comfortable.

On this same promontory, near the Treaty House, stands the *Whare-
Runanga* (Meeting House), a unique example of the great Maori meeting
houses around which the life of the old-time communities revolved. This
one is unique because its carvings are representative of all the tribes, with
each carved figure representing a tribal ancestor. The *tukutuku* work, a
kind of reed mosaic, which lines the walls, is exquisite, and the portrait
figures and the strange ancestor figures with their combination of human
and avian features, are amongst the finest in the land. Most such
buildings have names which are of tribal significance. This one, belonging
to no tribe but to the entire Maori race is simply Whare-Runanga, the
Meeting House.

Beside it is a long, low, carven shed housing a great Maori war canoe,
a splendid *wakataua* 33.76m (117ft) long, built of three great *kauri* trees
felled in the Puketi State Forest especially for the New Zealand Centen-
nial celebrations in 1940. The canoe was manned on that occasion by

A corner of Rewa's village at Kerikeri; this is a full-scale reconstruction of the kind of village the Maoris lived in before the Europeans came

80 paddlers, and sped across the harbour like a torpedo.

In the gentle, rolling hill country inland from the Bay of Islands is another charming old house, the Waimate North Mission, ("North" because there is another Waimate in the South Island), the first inland settlement established by Europeans. A brilliant Church of England missionary, Bishop Selwyn, first Anglican Bishop of New Zealand (and the last, but that is another story), made it his headquarters in 1842. Here the first Christian European marriage was solemnised. Today, the place looks much as it did in Bishop Selwyn's day, a little touch of civilised grace in the midst of what must have seemed an alien and strange land. The present church, built from the timber of a much larger church erected thirty-two years previously, is the third church to have been built here. The larger church served the Bishop as a cathedral – New Zealand's first – and as chapel of St John's College, a theological college established by Selwyn in 1843, to train men for ordination. The present Vicarage of Waimate North was built in 1832, and is the second oldest house in New Zealand.

Northward along the coast from Paihia is Kerikeri, where regular missionary activity had its earliest beginnings. Kerikeri was the home of that great Ngapuhi chieftain and uncle of Hone Heke, called Hongi Hika, often (and more probably) spelt Hongi Ika, a name which, in that form, may be translated as "He Who Smells Out the Fish", another way of saying "He Whose Enemies Never Escape". Hika, on the other hand, means "girl" and it is unlikely that any man dared call him that.

Hongi was one of the first Maoris to be taken to England – a rash thing, as it turned out. They took him because he was intelligent, and they thought he would be of some assistance to one Professor Lee of

Cambridge, who was compiling a simple Maori dictionary and grammar.

Hongi was feted in England. The king gave him a suit of armour which he had admired in the Tower of London, and thereafter the rich and resplendent vied with each other in giving him expensive presents, all of which, except the armour, he sold in Sydney on the way home, buying guns with the proceeds. When he got home, he led his tribesmen off on a trail of slaughter and destruction which took him as far south as the island of Mokoia, on Lake Rotorua, in the centre of the North Island. Here, the brave Arawa people, having only wood and stone weapons, were defeated, though they mauled Hongi's force so badly that he dragged his army home to Kerikeri, to lick its wounds and ponder on the inadvisability of walking into hornets' nests.

Professor Lee's dictionary and grammar proved useless.

Hongi's *pa* overlooked the beautiful, landlocked basin where the Kerikeri river flows out into the Bay of Islands. Here, in 1819, came Church of England missionaries, sent out by the Church Mission Society under the direction of the Rev. Samuel Marsden. Prepared to rough it, they nevertheless had every intention of setting an example of civilised living. Though preaching, teaching agriculture and giving the Maoris a general education, they found time, over a period, to erect New Zealand's first European house, built by the Rev. John Butler, who moved into it in 1822. Ten years later, after being occupied by several other families, it was taken over by lay preacher and blacksmith James Kemp, whose descendants occupied it for 142 years, until Kemp's great-grandson presented it to the New Zealand Historic Places Trust in 1974.

It is an interesting building, simple in design, intricate in construction. The framing is not nailed, but morticed together, and the weatherboarding is painstakingly tongue-and-grooved, by hand. The door panelling represents the Cross and an open Bible. The whole house sits on enormous 20.5cm (8in) by 10.2cm (4in) *kauri* floor plates resting on boulders.

Nearby, the old stone mission store is still in use, as a museum. Here, framed on the wall, is a copy of the first land deed, drawn up between the Revs John Butler and Thomas Kendal, and Hongi Ika – "Shungee Heeka, Chief of the District of Keddie Keddie". Over the fireplace are framed copies of letters written by James Kemp, typed out for easier reading. They tell of the difficulties faced by the missionaries and their families in those first years; of Maoris climbing over their fences and stealing their fruit and poultry, and manhandling anyone who remonstrated. (These were Hongi's people, though the missionaries lived under Hongi's protection. With a friend such as Hongi, who needed enemies?)

A little way up the hill from the basin, near the church – small, wooden and itself an architectural delight – is the first ground in New Zealand ever to feel the plough; and nearby, a road dips down to a pottery and what is probably the only specimen of a pre-European Maori *kainga* to be found in New Zealand today.

A *kainga* is a village, as opposed to a *pa*, and is surrounded by a palisade which is obviously designed to serve as a fence rather than a defence. The *kainga* has not the permanence of a *pa* or a larger community – Maoris sometimes lived in "cities" with up to 10,000 inhabitants – and most of its *whares* (houses) are simple, thatched dwellings, just high enough for a tall adult to sit or kneel upright in. The Maori spent little of his time indoors, and his dwelling was simply a place in which to sleep.

The village is not a true relic. Obviously, such dwellings would have rotted away long ago, for it is a long time since the Maoris lived in this simple fashion. It is, however, as authentic as painstaking research and considerable skill can make it – and it is particularly interesting to compare it with the villages of the ancient Celts in Britain, for instance.

Kerikeri is noted today for its fruit-growing, especially its citrus fruits,

Scene of a violent clash between Maori and *Pakeha* in 1809, when the *Boyd* was ransacked and burned, Whangaroa has long been a quiet haven for big-game fishermen

and every orchard seems to have its roadside stall. Even in winter they offer oranges, mandarin oranges, grapefruit, apples, papaws and tree tomatoes, known nowadays as tamarillos.

About 15 kilometres (9½ miles) from Kerikeri is Puketi State Forest, a *kauri* reserve. There are bigger trees in the Waipoua State Forest, but at Puketi they are displayed to better advantage. A long aisle has been cut to the foot of one old giant so that visitors can gaze up at him and see at one look his great height and the sculpted perfection of his massive trunk.

The Northern Harbours

North of Puketi is Kaeo, where the Wesleyans struggled to establish their mission in the face of the malice of Hori (George), Chief of the Whangaroa natives, and the mischief of Hongi's people. They eventually prevailed. The road runs through red clay country to Whangaroa. "Red Clay" insufficiently describes a volcanic soil which turns roadside embankments into palettes of delicate pinks and orange shadings.

Whangaroa means "Long Harbour", and the name describes it pretty well, for it meanders inland for about 12 kilometres (7½ miles), stretching lazy arms into indentations between grotesquely rock-crowned hills.

Whangaroa village, a loose grouping of comfortable old houses and a pub, world-famous as a big-game fishing base, clings to the shoreline at the foot of a great, rock-domed hill. The rock dome, a huge monolith known as St Paul's Cupola, is perfectly matched across the harbour by an identical dome inevitably known as St Peter's Cupola. In its heyday, Whangaroa was a timber port from which *kauri* was shipped. It has a fairly grim history in spite of its present-day peace and beauty, for it was from here that Hori's warriors sallied forth to loot and burn the Wesleyan Mission at Kaeo; and it was here that the sailing vessel *Boyd* was burnt

Pleasure craft bob gently on the smooth waters of Mangonui's secure and sheltered Doubtless Bay

and its crew massacred, because the captain had flogged a young Maori crew member, son of a local chief, for some misdemeanour, and the father and son decided to take *utu* – repayment. While looting the ship, a spark from a pipe was dropped in the powder magazine, and the ship blew up, killing many Maoris and burning the ship to the waterline. Her keel and ribs are still visible.

Unlike the majority of history's villains, the bloody-minded Hongi died peacefully of old age here at Whangaroa.

From Whangaroa, the road runs past shallow waterways and mudflats thick with mangrove to Mangonui, a quaintly delightful little period piece sited on a snug and landlocked harbour in the south-eastern corner of Doubtless Bay, at the point where the convex edge of the Maori knife fits into the handle.

The beauty of Mangonui – the name means "Big Shark" – is that it has kept its quaintness, its South Sea Island air, more or less intact. Its one and only street curves around a waterfront adorned with *pohutukawa*, and its general store backs away from the street to stand on stilts out over the water, its crowded window staring at the road, the hill face, and the pub. The pub, with that atmosphere, that elusive something which is made manifest in the Victorian dignity of its entrance hall, just a little bit richer than its position calls for, has the friendliest old bar imaginable, still solidly, unashamedly wooden, with shelves mercifully innocent of strips of coloured neon. It is likely to be slightly loud with a laughing group of Maoris playing English darts in a corner.

It's all an illusion, of course. The real town, the new town, the one with rose-coloured or pale green Summerhill stone houses and computerised petrol pumps, is just over the hill. But they've kept old Mangonui intact, perhaps just to have somewhere to slip back to when today's world becomes too pressing or strident.

According to Maori tradition, Cape Reinga, or at least the 800-year-old *pohutukawa* there, is the departure point for the spirits of the dead

Doubtless Bay, curving away to the north, sheltered by the enclosing arm of the Karikari peninsula, is a fast-developing beach resort. It was named by Captain Cook in his log on 19 December 1769: "... a deep Bay running SW by W and WSW, at the bottom of which we could but just see, and where the land appear'd to be low and level ... This Bay I have named Doubtless Bay; the wind not permitting us to look into this Bay, we steered for the Westernmost land we had in sight."

The "Westernmost land" was probably North Cape, one of the quartet of headlands northernmost in New Zealand, called North Cape, Hooper Point, Cape Reinga and Cape Maria van Diemen.

Cape Reinga and Ninety Mile Beach

Cape Reinga, according to Maori lore, is the departing place of the spirits of the dead. At the top of the Aupori Peninsula, it rears above Ninety Mile Beach, a steep complex of windswept, dun-coloured, grassy ridges and spurs. Ninety Mile Beach has a much finer name, now, alas, seldom if ever used. It used to be called One-roa-a-Tohea, which means "Tohea's Long Run", and refers to the feat of a warrior, Tohea, who, when his chief craved a meal of pigeons, ran the whole length of the beach, speared some fat birds, cooked them and delivered them to his chief, still hot. He did not have to run for 90 miles (145 kilometres), however. Or, rather, he did – 45 miles (72.5 kilometres) each way, which is the actual length of the beach.

Te One-roa-a-Tohea/Ninety Mile Beach is lapped by the Tasman Sea, and the eastern shore, a mere 6 kilometres (3½ miles) away at this point, is gnawed and licked by the Pacific Ocean. The two seas meet at Cape Reinga, the Pacific sweeping around North Cape and along the stepped curves of Tom Bowling and Spirits Bays to clash with the Tasman Sea in a welter of treacherous tides and fierce, conflicting currents beneath those steep hillsides and cliffs where the Cape Reinga Lighthouse cautions the ships which pass between Cape Reinga and Three Kings Islands.

The sea hereabouts is indeed dangerous, as the Maoris have known for generations. They have a legend – if you can call it that – that wherever a vessel sinks in the vicinity, the spot will be marked by a rainbow. It may sound quaint, or even laughable; but the hard fact remains that when a collier capsized and sank in the weird seas off the Cape a few years ago, Maoris pointed out a persistent rainbow near a submerged sandbank, and though nobody took much notice, the wreckage was eventually found there, by the use of divers, echo-sounding equipment, and all the gimmicks with which a zealous but sceptical science has equipped us.

Most of this Mangonui County, including the Aupori Peninsula, was once a gumfield, to which thronged diggers from all over the world. In the sandy soil of the peninsula, gum is still found in workable quantities, and the best grades still fetch a high price. For this reason there are still odd old characters in the area, silent, self-sufficient men who dig for *kauri* gum with long, spear-like probes and with spades, and who seem to have a spiritual kinship with the gold fossickers in the desert states of America.

Mangamuka and Hokianga Harbour

South of Kaitaia, where the road gradually climbs up along ridges from which *kauri* forest falls away from the road into dreaming valleys of greenery, is the lovely Mangamuka Gorge, from which the way passes around the head of the Hokianga Harbour. As it winds its peaceful way past the brown hills, the inlet is navigable for shallow-draught vessels

White-gold sands, stretching to the far horizon, characterise Ninety Mile Beach,
also famous for the quantities of that gastronomic delicacy, *toheroa*, found there

to the very heart of the Northland peninsula.

Hokianga Harbour was another spot favoured by the first settlers of both races and it was in this vicinity that one Baron de Thierry attempted to set up an independent kingdom on 40,000 acres of land, described in an extremely shaky Deed as "the district called Tetu One, at the source or rise of the River Yokianga, the District called Te Papa, all of which districts are situated at the source, on the eastern and western banks of the River Yokianga, and contain by estimation 40,000 acres, the same more or less, and all woods and waters, and whatever may be contained and situated within the aforesaid boundaries...". He bought the land – or thought he had – for 36 axes. The Maoris disputed this, and actually offered him a smaller parcel of land, about 5,000 acres, near Kohukohu on the western bank (which is really the northern bank) of the "Yokianga River", which turned out to be Hokianga Harbour. He was a man of large ideas, but the immigrants he brought with him did not share de Thierry's vision. Nor were the missionaries or the Government anxious to see a sovereign state set up, even one so small. So the whole idea came to nothing.

Hokianga Harbour's steep hills shelter, on the northern side, the little village of Kohukohu, and on the southern side, the steep little township of Rawene; and down near the mouth, where great, tawny sandhills lie like a pride of gigantic, somnolent lions across the calm water, Opononi and its twin resort Omapere drowse on a shore of haunting beauty. Their beaches are dazzling white, and the hills surrounding them are patched with bush. Here, in the summer of 1955–56, a friendly dolphin took up residence and became a tremendous favourite, especially with the children, with whom she played tirelessly. They rode on her back, played ball with her and loved her. People wrote stories about her, and even a popular song. And for one whole, long, glorious summer, the whole country read about her and listened eagerly for news items about her and shared vicariously the delight of the holiday crowds at Opononi in the captivating charm of the graceful trusting creature. And when Opo (as they called her) died (and it is whispered strongly that some mindless or heartless person shot her) at the end of that enchanted summer, the whole country mourned her passing.

There's a monument to her there, a charming statue of Opo gambolling in the water with a small boy.

Waipoua State Forest, Dargaville and Matakohe

Southward from Opononi and Omapere, the countryside begins to take on, once more, a Mangamuka-like beauty, and presently the road runs into Waipoua State Forest, last kingdom of the lordly *kauri*. The great, pale boles are suggestive of those Cedars of Lebanon from which Solomon made the pillars of his Temple. At one (signposted) point, a footway leads into the forest, to the great *kauri* Tane Mahuta, "The God of the Forest", estimated to be 1,200 years old. He is, even now, by no means senile. Muscular is the word he calls to mind as he stands there in the fullness and pride of his mighty strength. Over 13.7m (45ft) around his middle, with his lowest branches about 12.6m (41ft 6ins) from the ground, he is fenced in, standing on a small mound, his full height visible from outside the enclosure.

There is another, comparable tree in the Waipoua State Forest. Te Matua Ngahere, "The Father of the Forest", has a 16m (53ft) girth. He is not such a straight and perfect specimen as Tane Mahuta, but he is, for all that, a lordly creature.

South of Waipoua State Forest is Dargaville, once the northern terminus for the shipping which plied the Kaipara Harbour. The main road to Dargaville from Waipoua bypasses another *kauri* reserve, Trounson Kauri Park, a block of about seven acres in the Kaihu valley, in which

Beautiful Opononi on Hokianga Harbour, where Opo the dolphin played during the summer of 1955–6

stand more giants. In times past, it contained trees beside which Tane Mahuta would have been a mere stripling, a mere callow youth. One of these, destroyed by fire, had a girth of 24m (78ft), and its giant limbs may still be seen scattered on the ground, any one of them as big as a sizeable tree.

Dargaville was the first place in New Zealand in which a Yugoslav Consulate was set up, to watch the interests of a large colony of Dalmatians in the area. They had arrived in the 1850s from the peninsula of Peljesac on the coast of the Republic of Ragusa (Dubrovnik), and, by dint of much hard work and exemplary citizenship, became a generally prosperous people, industrious and prominent in civic affairs. The family names, ending in the characteristic "ich" syllable, are to be seen everywhere. They are, in their speech, indistinguishable from other New Zealanders, but they have retained some of their customs, and their festivals and gatherings are colourful. They have contributed greatly to

the now-flourishing winemaking industry in New Zealand.

Dargaville was one of the principal timber ports in the days when this region was covered in forest. The Wairoa river, in which vessels of up to 10,000 tons have anchored, was once the scene of monumental log jams, when it was possible to walk dryfoot across the river on log rafts packed tightly from bank to bank.

The coast is a short distance from the town. Baylys Beach is a long and wild stretch of quite beautiful beach, site of many ancient Maori *pas* and *kaingas*. The remains of *hangis* – a type of oven – and *tokis*, which are stone axes, are still often found. The Maoris favoured the location because of the fishing, which was excellent, and because of the abundant supply of *toheroa*, which are a type of clam, highly esteemed by gourmets, especially in soup, which is claimed to rival turtle soup.

The long beaches are often windswept and wild, and shifting sandbanks wander up and down the coast. There have been many wrecks over the years, and the sands still hide the wreckage of two ships, the French thirty-six, *L'Alcemène*, and what is thought to be a Portuguese caravel. Occasionally portions of them are displayed, such as a well-preserved bow, or sections of a timbered hull, only to be quickly whisked away again within a few hours.

The road from Dargaville meanders south around the harbour, through Naumai, which means "Welcome", and which was once a regular wayport for Kaipara shipping; and through Raupo, named after a bulrush reed growing profusely hereabouts; and Ruawai, which means "Waterhole".

It climbs away inland from the harbour to Matakohe, a small settlement but one not to be missed, because it possesses a special treasure. Near the attractive little Coates Memorial Church, dedicated to the memory of Joseph Gordon Coates, the country's first New Zealand-born Prime Minister, is the superb Pioneer Museum, housing very fine pioneer-period photographs and the world-famous J.J. Lord Collection, the country's largest single collection of *kauri* gum. It is a treasure-trove, all gold and amber, translucent and lovely, spread out and illuminated so that, like Northland itself, it offers sublime beauty for easy viewing.

The giant *kauri*, Tane Mahuta, "God of the Forest", soars above the surrounding trees in the Waipoua State Forest

An aerial view of Auckland, New Zealand's largest city, with the 1020-m (3348-ft) Harbour Bridge over Waitemata Harbour in the foreground

Auckland

Queen Street bisects the busy centre of Auckland, running from the city's main dock area on the Waitemata Harbour south-west to Newton

Some cities, perhaps most old-world cities, seem to have just grown, from fortification sites, market gathering places, ancient ports; or perhaps they are settlements of incredible antiquity whose sites were chosen originally because the area was favourable for settlement.

Auckland was intended from the first to be a city.

Indeed, a surveyor-planner was brought over from Sydney, Australia, for the specific purpose of planning the place. Unfortunately, he was rather fonder of the grog shops which were already there than he was of his instruments and his drawing board. He presently submitted a beautiful plan, incorporating well-conceived circuses, avenues, boulevards and terraces, which his masters admired greatly. Unhappily, attempts to execute the plan resulted in a confusion of queer little streets and cul-de-sacs: the Tamaki Isthmus on which the city was to be built was very hilly, whereas his plan was flat. Unhappily, that is, for those who had to try to build to his scheme, but most happily for posterity; for the odd little lanes, stairwayed terraces and wandering streets make Auckland a cheerfully informal, happily livable city.

Of course the plan was adjusted, this time by a planner whose mind was on the job; but the settlers who were already there couldn't wait, and went ahead, doing their best with sections placed on the precipitous slopes of the thirty-seven extinct volcanoes on which Auckland was sited. Queen Street, the main commercial thoroughfare, had to be laid out a little to the south and a little to the north of the place provided in the plan, which turned out to be a deep gully, shrub-filled and gouged by a brawling stream.

None of this seemed to worry anyone unduly. From the beginning, Aucklanders were an optimistic, slightly happy-go-lucky bunch. Their town was founded, in a brisk and navy-like manner, by Captain William Hobson, an officer sent to New Zealand as Lieutenant-Governor. Towards the end of 1840, less than a month after choosing the site and paying for it – 3,000 acres for 50 blankets, £50 in cash, 20 pairs of trousers, 20 shirts, 10 waistcoats, 10 caps, 4 casks of tobacco, 1 box of pipes, 100 yards of gown pieces, 10 iron pots, 1 bag of sugar, 1 bag of flour and 20 hatchets as a down-payment – Hobson had "the officers of the Government and the mechanics and labourers under their orders, proceeding with the necessary works for establishing the town which I contemplate being the future seat of Government, and which I purpose distinguishing by the name of 'Auckland'." (The name was a prudent choice. As Hobson wrote to his wife in 1836, "many a valuable officer pines in obscurity merely because he has no friends to bring his merits to notice". Hobson had friends, of whom one of the foremost was Lord Auckland.)

On the arrival of the ship carrying the new settlers, the town was inaugurated with the raising of the Union Jack, Her Majesty's health being drunk at the foot of the flagstaff, and three times three hearty British cheers from the assembly. They then held a regatta, with ships' boats and a Maori canoe competing for a purse of guineas.

Even so, Auckland had to be brought to birth by hard, slogging work, grim determination and the unquenchable optimism of some seventy-five men, women and children. It is not altogether surprising, therefore, that Auckland has been described as a city built on "blind faith and thirty-seven extinct volcanoes". (Incidentally, this statement is inaccurate. Faith is seldom as blind as it seems; and at least some of the volcanoes are not extinct, but merely dormant.)

The heart, if not the precise geometrical centre of Auckland is the main shopping concourse, Queen Street, lively, crowded and colourful for over half of its two-kilometre (mile and a quarter) length, the upper reaches of which are less commercially slick but rather more endearing, with shabby antique and curiosity shops, close to where it runs into Karangahape Road, which crosses the top of Queen Street like a bent,

Auckland's War Memorial Museum stands in the parkland of Auckland Domain
and houses superb collections of New Zealand and South Pacific artefacts

rakish, slightly disreputable bar on a capital T.

Karangahape Road is a colourful street, too, a bargain-basement
reflection of Queen Street, more happy-go-lucky, decidedly Polynesian,
rather friendlier, running between Pitt Street and Symonds Street. At its
Symonds Street end the crowds seem to thin out with almost magical
abruptness, and there is a tree-shaded and quiet Jewish cemetery, right
there on one of Auckland's main business thoroughfares!

This is an Auckland peculiarity, and one of the city's greatest charms,
this frequency of odd little oases, like Myers Park, which drops down
anonymously behind Karangahape Road's shops, a strip of comfortable
green lawns and phoenix palms sandwiched between the tall and sightless
backs of commercial buildings and opening on to Queen Street just
behind the Town Hall.

Crossing frantic Symonds Street, you can walk to the Grafton Bridge,
beneath which runs the even more frantic Motorway. The Motorway
displaced the long-undisturbed Grafton Gully bush and, with it, many of
the graves of the pioneers, who are now remembered by plaques on either
side of Symonds Street, nineteenth-century susceptibilities preserved in
the careful arrangement of Anglicans on one side, Catholics on the other.
The grave of the city's father, Captain William Hobson, has fortunately
been preserved. He died on 10 September 1842, aged 49, and on each
anniversary a commemoration ceremony is held at the graveside.

Across Grafton Bridge, in Park Street, an ornamental gateway gives
on to Auckland Domain, perhaps one of the two most beautiful parks in
the Dominion. It is an area of lawns, gardens, sports fields and scenic
drives, draped carefully over the city's hilly heart. At the top of its central
hill stands the War Memorial Museum, approached by flights of broad
steps which climb past the Cenotaph with its furled flags – consecrated
ground from which naval guns stare out, forever silent, across the
harbour. Within the Museum is the Hall of Memories, a flag-hung shrine
in which are inscribed the names of all who went forth from Auckland
Province to die in foreign wars.

The Museum's ethnological and anthropological room is particularly
impressive, especially its Maori exhibits, including the great 25m (82ft)
war canoe, *Toki-a-Tapiri* ("Tapiri's Axe"), which was captured in Manukau Harbour at the start of the Kingite Wars in the 1860s, where it was

A trigonometrical station for Auckland province now tops the cone of the extinct volcano, Mount Eden, where for centuries the Maoris had a *pa*

one of the Maoris' war fleet and a principal means of communication.

Of all the thirty-seven volcanoes on which Auckland, out-Romeing Rome, was built, the two most famous are Mount Eden and One Tree Hill. Mount Eden is a suburb, south of and fairly close to the city centre. The hill's volcanic origins are apparent, not only in the shape of the cone, but also in the scoria fences and walls which are so common in the vicinity. The actual peak from which the suburb takes its name is an almost perfectly symmetrical volcanic cone complete with a deep crater in its 195m (643ft) summit. This crater is perfectly circular and, like the Whispering Gallery in the dome of London's St Paul's Cathedral, has interesting acoustical properties. Its other remarkable feature is that although it is plainly an ancient crater, grassed over from top to bottom, frost never forms on the bottom even when the surrounding ground is white with it.

The view from its summit is superb, with the city spread out below, and the harbour and the Hauraki Gulf beyond, with its numerous islands stretching into the distance. A plane table indicates points of interest.

The sides of the cone are terraced, a sure indication that this hill was once a strongly fortified *pa*, and the ground is dotted with shallow

The obelisk on One Tree Hill, another extinct volcano, was erected to mark Sir John Logan Campbell's admiration for the Maoris; his grave is nearby

depressions which were once storage pits for *kumara* (sweet potatoes) and other foodstuffs for the garrison. Many a bloody battle was fought about Mount Eden in pre-European times.

One Tree Hill, farther out from the centre of town, in the suburb of Green Lane, south-east of Mount Eden, is another ancient fortress site. Today it bears at its summit, in place of the original *totàra* tree which gave it its name, and which was cut down by vandals, a memorial to John Logan Campbell, an energetic doctor-turned-businessman who did much to promote the prosperity of the once struggling little community, and bring it to city status. Nearby stands a tall obelisk, erected as a tribute to the Maori race; and at the foot of One Tree Hill stands Campbell's old wooden cottage, built in 1843, and now preserved and furnished as a pioneer museum. There is, incidentally, a replacement tree on the hill.

East of One Tree Hill, at the base of a long finger of land forming the eastern shore of a tidal inlet reaching south from the Hauraki Gulf, the so-called Tamaki river, is Howick. Here, in the late 1840s, three companies of a veterans' corps, known as the Royal New Zealand Fencibles, were settled by Sir George Grey, then Governor of New Zealand, for the defence of Auckland against hostile Maoris in the nearby Wairoa Ranges, and canoe-borne parties from the Firth of Thames, across the Hauraki Gulf. Fencibles were given land, cottages and some financial assistance, in return for which they kept themselves drilled and at readiness to drop their ploughs and take up their muskets as a trained military band. The name of their settlement was taken from

McDermott Cottage, a "fencible" cottage for two families built near Auckland
in 1848 and now carefully restored

Howick Hall in Northumberland, Earl Grey's seat.

There is a splendid Colonial Museum and reconstructed Fencible
Cottage at Howick, with fine relics from the colonial period. Also here is
the very lovely little All Saints Church, designed by the missionary, the
Rev. Frederick Thatcher, who had trained as an architect. All Saints is
one of a number of churches built by Bishop Selwyn, whose diocese was
the entire country plus the distant Chatham Islands, no mean territory in
the days when there were virtually no roads, and most travelling was done
on foot through dense forest and along the coast, on horseback when the
nature of the country allowed it, and by sea and up rivers by schooner.
The churches with which he dotted the country, known as the Selwyn
Churches, are small architectural gems, of which All Saints is held by
many to be the prize.

From St Heliers on the eastern edge of Auckland, the incomparable
Tamaki Drive runs westward along the harbour's edge, starting at St
Heliers Bay, (named by homesick settlers from the Channel Islands after
St Helier in Jersey), and running through Mission Bay, where, in 1859,
Bishop Selwyn built a school for Melanesian students. St John's College,
the existing theological college, was found to be on too bleak and cold a
site for these young men from the tropics. The father of John Coleridge
Patteson, first Bishop of Melanesia (who was to die a martyr's death in
that territory), contributed largely to the cost, and the authoress Charlotte Yonge set aside the whole of the proceeds of her book, *The Daisy
Chain*, for the building fund. Bishop Patteson was consecrated at the

college, and as part of the celebration, the Norfolk pines, which grow like giant Christmas trees around the bay, were planted. The college has long since been transferred to Norfolk Island.

Between St Heliers and Mission Bay spreads Kohimarama Beach, a cradle of New Zealand aviation, where two brothers named Walsh established a flying school in the years immediately before World War I. Land in the vicinity of Auckland being expensive, and flat land at a special premium, the Walsh Brothers opted for float planes, the (more or less) flat waters of the harbour being free and unencumbered.

From Mission Bay the road runs around Bastion Point, past the concrete ramparts of a fortification no longer in warlike use, whose ammunition magazine forms the sepulchre of a beloved New Zealand Premier, Michael Joseph Savage.

In a shallow indentation on the point is the anchorage of the Tamaki Yacht Club; and in the next two bays, sheltered by a long mole, is Easthaven Boat Harbour, headquarters of the Royal Akarana Yacht Club. In these two broad havens, a vast number of yachts, launches and other pleasure craft are moored, a convincing indication of Aucklanders' love affair with their beautiful harbour.

Turning south from where Tamaki Drive becomes the busy thorough-fare of Quay Street, main route to the docks, a network of streets resolves itself into the suburb of Parnell, one of Auckland's oldest. Hereabouts is Parnell Village, a restoration, a charming conversation piece, a respite from the aggressive modernity and brash commercialism of the Queen Street-Karangahape Road region. Its wooden shops with ornate Victorian and Edwardian curlicues, its cobblestones, its multi-paned shop windows, its verandas and stairways with turned wood posts and banisters, its air of fresh-painted colonial elegance, is endearingly nostalgic. But its greatest charm lies in the fact that this is no musty museum piece, redolent of mothballs and ancient dust, but a vibrantly alive corner of Auckland. The shops, the restaurants, are in business, and business is brisk, in a leisurely, comfortable way.

On the western side of the city, alongside the Great North Road, is Western Springs. Once the city's reservoir, it is now the Museum of Transport and Technology, close by Auckland Zoo, the country's largest

Above: Perhaps more colourful than colonial Auckland ever was, Parnell
Village's carefully preserved old houses offer charming glimpses into the city's past
Opposite: The spinnakers are up as these yachts sail on the Waitemata Harbour off
Rangitoto Island

St Stephen's Chapel, Judges Bay, Parnell, *c.* 1856. The Constitution of the
Church of England Province of New Zealand was signed here in 1857

and one of its finest. The Giraffe Slide and Willow Castle, packed with
fairytale characters, hippos, dragons and pelicans, are charming and
practical drawcards for smaller children who, understandably, can be very
bored by sleepy and immobile polar bears, lions and tigers.

Though the centre of Auckland is unrelentingly commercial with its
highrise steel and glass and concrete towers, and the newer eastern
suburbs are determinedly business-executive-modern in style, much of the
colonial past still stands sturdily; as, for example, another of the charming
Selwyn churches, St Stephen's Chapel in Judges Bay, as nineteenth-
century as a poke bonnet, maintaining an almost timeless, unassailable
peace against a raucous background of wharves and warehouses, derricks
and cargo vessels. Like All Saints in Howick, it is built of wood. Not all
of the Selwyn churches are; the simple, pleasing and beautifully balanced
St James' Church at Mangere, erected in 1840 and now not far from

Auckland University's extravagantly Gothic Clock Tower looks out over Albert Park in the centre of the city

Auckland International Airport, is built of stone.

Otherwise, Auckland offers little enough of architectural consequence. There is quite a lot of pleasing domestic architecture, from the genuinely colonial to the fussily Victorian, and sometimes an engaging combination of both, such as Alberton, on Mount Albert Road. Built in 1862, it was originally a farmhouse in the pleasing wooden colonial-Victorian gabled style, with a strong kinship with houses built in England for a similar purpose. A generation later, it was dressed all around with towers and verandas which were plainly influenced by Indian architecture, and suggest Imperial pride.

For sheer architectural *joi-de-vivre*, perhaps the prime example is the University's wedding-cake tower, a positive flirtation of Gown with Town, cheerful, uncharacteristically extravagant amongst all the stern Gothic Revival, and lovable.

Auckland's Harbour Bridge, built in 1959 to link the city's centre with its northern suburbs. The wings were added later to give the bridge eight lanes

The peninsula which sprawls across the northern side of the harbour, in shape vaguely like a clenched fist with a pointing index finger, is Waitemata County. Spread across its hills and dales are the boroughs of Birkenhead, Northcote and Devonport, nostalgically named by the earliest settlers after sadly-missed homes, and the City of Takapuna, whose name signifies a water spring under a knoll.

The County is reached by way of the Harbour Bridge, which is one of those engineering miracles which, not so many years ago, used to rank with the Seven Wonders of the World, but which today are accepted with a casual shrug. The bridge is 1020.5m (3348ft) long, with the main span 243.9m (800ft) in length, clearing the water at high tide by 43.3m (142ft). Originally 12.8m (42ft) wide, with four traffic lanes, it was later widened by the addition of wings to each side, increasing traffic capacity to eight lanes. The wings, erected by a Japanese engineering company, are irreverently known as the "Nippon Clipon". The stretch of water over which the bridge strides is the site of the oldest one-day regatta in the world, the water over which those ships' boats and Maori canoes competed for Hobson's golden guineas. The same stretch is raced over each Anniversary Day, in commemoration – and, of course, for the sheer fun of the thing.

Northcote is a picturesque suburb, with banana trees growing in domestic gardens, and Norfolk pines and *pohutukawas* in its public reserves. Takapuna, on the pointing "forefinger", is endowed with a splendour of sandy beaches, including the long, golden sweeps of Takapuna Beach, St Leonards Beach, Narrow Neck and Cheltenham Beach, bordering the Rangitoto Channel and sheltered by the flat cone of Rangitoto Island. On the southern tip of the finger is Devonport, built about its naval dockyard. At the base of the peninsula, which pokes its deeply indented length into Waitemata Harbour, is Lake Pupuke, whose full name is Pupukemoana, which means "Overflowing Sea", so named because it spills its springs out across the sea beach. It is a crater of awesome

Takapuna Beach, one of the finest of the many glorious beaches along
Auckland's North Shore

depth, the waters of which, though it is within 200m (650ft) of the sea,
are absolutely fresh. It is the spring from which Takapuna takes its name.

Incidentally, "Waitemata", Auckland Harbour's name, is held to
mean "Sparkling Waters". In fact, the name means "Smooth Waters", or,
more fully, "Waters as smooth as obsidian".

To the west of Auckland lies Henderson, famous for its vineyards –
especially the longest standing, famous Mount Lebanon Vineyards, named
after his homeland by Assid Abraham Corban, an immigrant who brought
to New Zealand a 300-years-old tradition of winemaking.

South-west of Henderson are the Waitakere Ranges, forest-clad, beautiful, here and there concealing some of Auckland's finest and most beautiful homes, and offering an enchanting selection of bush walks, astonishing on the edge of such an intensely urban sprawl.

Beyond the Waitakere Ranges is the west coast, and a remarkable series of curved and sandy beaches, where a river slips out from between the Waitakeres' feet to stain the sea with silt; and a lazy piece of natural sculpture called Lion Rock sprawls at the mouth of the Piha Stream, which gives its name to this lovely, spectacular stretch of wild coast.

Manukau Harbour, on the south side of Auckland, is shallow, and not now of any commercial importance, though in colonial times it used to be busy with coastal trade. Vessels of comparatively shallow draught used to brave the bar at its entrance and dock at Onehunga, just across the water from the Mangere Peninsula, where Auckland's International Airport is now situated. It was in this harbour that the great Maori war canoe, *Toki-a-Tapiri*, was captured at the beginning of the Kingite War in 1863.

In those days, the forces of the Maori King planned to overwhelm Auckland and drive the resented white man, the *Pakeha*, into the sea. But they didn't, and Auckland, delivered from catastrophe, received its first real population boost from Australia, where men enlisted in forces brought over to fight in the war, and stayed to build this sprawling, cheerful, somewhat raucous city which, increasingly Polynesian though it is, is still more akin to Sydney and to Australia generally than to any other city in New Zealand.

Hauraki Gulf

Auckland is the base for excursions into the Hauraki Gulf, the nearest of whose fascinating collection of islands is that same Rangitoto, the flattened cone which rises just across the channel from Takapuna. Newest of all Auckland's volcanic cones, it is still largely a scrub-covered waste of jagged volcanic rock.

It is almost in the grip of the crab-claw shaped Motutapu ("Sacred Island"), which appears to be rising up out of the waters of the Gulf to drag Rangitoto down to some lair beneath the sea. On Motutapu are two forts, one a magnificent example of an ancient Maori *pa*, the other a grass-grown, lonely place of concrete bunkers, decaying, vandal-smashed buildings and steps that go down to immovable doors behind which tunnels must still reach back into the very skeleton of the hills – a World War II fort, protecting the mouth of Waitemata Harbour. Motutapu is joined to Rangitoto by a slim thread of causeway.

Waiheke Island, 26 kilometres (16 miles) long by about 8 kilometres (5 miles) wide at its widest point, basks in the blue gulf waters about 16 kilometres (10 miles) across the Tamaki Strait from the mainland. Its hilly bulk, sandy beaches and ribbons of road lurk at the back of many a hard-working Kiwi's mental eyeball for thirty or forty years. He recalls it amid the sweat and dust of a summer sheepyard or the chafing confinement of office or shop as the place to which he will retire when at last he straightens his back and lays down his tools for good. He buys a small but pleasant dwelling, a dinghy or a launch according to the size of the fruits of his lifetime's toil, and lives happily in Cowes, or Oneroa ("Long Beach"), or Onetangi ("Mourning Beach"), or Palm Beach; and life lengthens and is warmly, drowsily pleasant, or perhaps is filled with a fresh phase of industry, like running a newspaper, or spinning wool, on

The impressive Lion Rock, sculpted by wind and water, marks where the Piha Stream reaches the sea at Piha Beach, west of the Waitakere Ranges

Port Fitzroy is the main settlement on Great Barrier Island, so-called by Captain Cook because it appeared to bar the way into the Hauraki Gulf

Waiheke – whose name means "Cascading Waters".

Faint and far away on the horizon is Little Barrier Island, a bird sanctuary which may be visited by special permission by genuine naturalists or ornithologists. Access is by a small amphibian aircraft from Auckland. The island is home to *kiwis*, *tuis*, the stitchbird, fantails, bellbirds, bush owls, and that last, living member of the dinosaur family, the *tuatara*, commonly growing to a length of .610m (2ft) and living to a hundred and fifty or more years. (One at least was known to the Maoris in modern times to have lived for three hundred years.)

Rugged Great Barrier Island, 90 kilometres (56 miles) north-eastward from Auckland, is the largest of the North Island's numerous off-shore islands. About 40 kilometres (25 miles) long and some 16 kilometres (10 miles) wide, it reaches a height of 621m (2038ft). There are many inlets and bays, and its principal settlements are Port Fitzroy, Tryphena (the biggest) and Okupu. All are pleasant places to stay, with guesthouse

The Mansion House built by Governor Sir George Gray on Kawau Island, and now a museum, is still surrounded by many of the exotic trees he imported

accommodation. Near Okupu are hot springs. Sheep farming is the main industry, and some beekeeping is carried on.

Kawau Island is a leading New Zealand resort, with numerous delightful bays, including Vivian Bay, North Cove, Bon Accord Harbour, South Cove, Bonsanquet Bay, Two House Bay and, of course, Mansion House Bay.

One of the smallest of the Gulf Islands, and the latest to be developed, is Pakatoa, a tiny islet off the coast of Waiheke, site of a delightful luxury resort.

These are the main tourist spots among the many islands in the Gulf; others are not always readily accessible. The islands mentioned provide all the characteristic features of the Gulf islands: the rocky, humped, brown beauty of hilly islands, the curving, perfect white-sand bays, the glory of *pohutukawa* fringing with scarlet the surf-white shores, and the dark, forest-draped heights.

Coromandel, once the scene of a frantic scramble for *kauri*, gum and gold, is a quiet place today

Coromandel and the
Bay of Plenty

Above: Thames, spreading along the Firth of Thames, has exchanged its old gold-mining activities for modern light industry
Opposite: Whitianga Harbour, on the east coast of the Coromandel Peninsula, is a popular holiday spot and a base for big-game fishermen

The Hauraki Gulf is bounded on its eastern side by the Coromandel peninsula, which reaches northward from the township of Thames, terminating in Cape Colville and the tiny settlement of Port Jackson. Thames sits on the south-eastern coast of the Firth of Thames, into which, oddly enough, no River Thames flows. It used to. Captain Cook sailed HMS *Endeavour* into the southern reaches of the Hauraki Gulf on 16 November 1769. He had himself rowed a short distance up the river which spilled out into the Gulf, named it Thames after that most famous of English rivers, and called this lower reach of the gulf in which he had anchored Firth of Thames. The latter name has stuck, but the river resumed its Maori name, Waihou, which means "New Water".

Today, the township of Thames is headquarters for a commercial fishing industry, but still possesses a few interesting old wooden pubs and wooden, false-fronted shops, relics of a lusty, goldmining past.

The road which leaves Thames and heads northward up the long, curving coast of the Coromandel peninsula makes royal progress, lined with beautiful, gnarled, extremely ancient *pohutukawa* trees, crimson with blossom in summer. A few of the little holiday settlements, small and companionable clusters of houses and stores fronting on to strips of white sand, were once important goldmining settlements, but all are now simply places to which people come to spend their leisure, or settle to lead self-sufficient lives subsisting happily on arts and crafts. For here the climate is wonderful, the sea warm and the fishing very good.

About the point where the Firth of Thames ceases to be the firth, and becomes the seaward Hauraki Gulf, the way turns inland, through hills which tower to dizzy heights above the Gulf, topped with castle-like rock pinnacles. Presently the road drops down again into a fertile valley lying

at the head of a mangrove-fringed bay known as Coromandel Harbour.
Coromandel, the town after which the peninsula was named, derived its
name from HMS *Coromandel*, a naval vessel which used to visit this
haven regularly for spars. For many years, Coromandel was the most
important goldmining settlement in the country, site of a fabulous reef
which was first discovered on 2 September 1867, and finally petered out
almost a hundred years later. At the height of its golden prosperity, some
8000 souls lived and laboured in the vicinity. A very accurate picture of
what it was like can be gained from the little School of Mines Museum.
There is still one quartz-crushing battery in Coromandel, sitting in a
corrugated iron shed at the foot of Tokatea Hill. No longer in use, it is
kept in working order, perhaps in the hope that gold will be rediscovered
in the vicinity, Coromandel will be revitalized to the point where it will
once again have umpteen dozen pubs, and the old suburb of Toptown will
spring from the bracken and scrub like a phoenix from the ashes.

Over the picturesque Coromandel Range, where the road climbs and
winds through forests which include fine stands of *kauri*, and vast stands
of *manuka* scrub which flowers in spring, its tangy scent mingling with the
cool fragrance of damp fern by the roadside, is Whitianga. The name is a
contraction of Whitianga-a-Kupe, meaning "The Crossing Place of Kupe".
An indefatigable explorer-navigator, Kupe left some members of his
expedition here as settlers. His visit was the beginning of human habitation in the area, over 1000 years ago. Kupe named several localities,
including a headland which juts out from the 3.5-kilometre (2-mile)
stretch of Buffalo Beach, which he called Te Wahine Moeroa ki Tapu
Tapuatea, which means "The Sacred Temple Where the Lady Slept
Forever". If ever a name promised a story, this one does; but it was, in

fact, the name of Kupe's temple on the island of Ra'iatea, about 165 kilometres (100 miles) from Tahiti.

Eventually, the descendants of Kupe's party raised a *pa*, on a rock which rises perpendicularly out of the water at the mouth of the Whitianga river. Little remains of it but a shallow indentation marking the site of a defensive ditch on the landward side. Captain Cook, writing of it in 1769, said: ". . . the situation is such that the best engineer in Europe could not have chosen a better site for a small number of men to defend against a greater". He figured that at some time not long before he first saw it, it had been taken by an enemy. But he was wrong. It was never taken, but abandoned. Since large bodies of enemy could simply ignore it, crossing the river at will to help themselves to all and everything that the defenders held valuable in the surrounding countryside, its use was limited to that of a place of refuge; and there are some things which a people of spirit value more highly than mere safety.

The land itself, for instance. On the western side of the Whitianga river, the present-day township spreads itself easily around the stretch of golden sand called Buffalo Beach, after HMS *Buffalo*, which was wrecked here in 1840. At the far end of the beach, the road climbs up over Te Wahine Moeroa ki Tapu Tapuatea and promptly degenerates into a dusty, winding, gravelled road which leads over the bush-patched hills to more beautiful and largely unfrequented beaches and bays, and to hamlets with

Above: Cook's Beach beyond Shakespeare Cliffs on Mercury Bay: anchored here
in November 1769, Captain Cook took possession of New Zealand for the
British Crown
Opposite: At Hot Water Beach hot springs exist beneath the sands: dig down
before high tide covers them and you may take a hot mineral bath

names like Kuaotunu and Te Rerenga. Here the hills march right down to
the water's edge, concealing lovely little flats and stretches of sand, and
enclosing golden bays in towering walls of dark forest.

Shakespeare Cliff, east of Whitianga township, across the river, was
named by Cook after a white cliff near Dover, England. It is a high
headland which curves its protective arm around Cooks Beach, the other
end of which is bounded by a zig-zagging tidal inlet and sheltered by a
higher, larger headland called Cooks Bluff. On a sunny day, the colours
of sea, headland and sky are glorious, a subtle blending of blues and
greens, white-flecked and gold-bordered, with a glowing palette of colour
in the clear, fierce ocean light which is itself a feature of this glorious
coast. In the distance, 10 kilometres (6 miles) across Mercury Bay (also
named by Cook, whose visit here in 1769 was to observe the transit of
Mercury), is the hazy hump of Opito Point, and some 20 kilometres (12
miles) distant rises the dark bulk of Great Mercury Island.

South of Whitianga, down a side road from Whenuakite, is Hot
Water Beach, where the sand is smooth and golden and the sea a startling
blue, with a good surf. The beach is backed by caverned cliffs topped with
native forest, and a shallow stream burbles over the sand and fans out
over the last wet width to mingle unobtrusively with the foam-flecked lip
of the sea. Here, at low tide, steam rises from the volcanic sands, and by

scooping a hole in the sand it is possible to enjoy a hot mineral bath – no formal, enclosed, architecturally marshalled spa, but a mineral bath of the kind the Maoris knew, out in the open, with the cool sea on one side and the bird-loud bush on the other.

Oddly, in this almost sub-tropical paradise, penguins have a colony a few miles to the south, and may often be seen darting and diving amongst the off-shore waves.

Along this coast, and particularly in Mercury Bay, big-game fishing is excellent, with fine specimens of black marlin, striped marlin, *mako* shark, thresher shark, tuna and kingfish being caught. Tuna are more numerous in these waters than anywhere else around New Zealand shores. Crayfish also abound here, particularly the variety known as "Packhorse", which not infrequently weigh up to 10kg (20lbs).

From Coroglen southward down the eastern side of the peninsula, the road is hilly, narrow and dusty. Yet it is very beautiful country, with magnificent seascapes glimpsed from high saddles and spurs. The road comes down to the coast again at Tairua, which means "Two Tides", and is probably a reference to the rough confusion of the water at the entrance to Tairua Harbour, due to tide, wind, ocean current and the flow of the Tairua river.

From Hikuai, which is the head of navigation on the Tairua, there is a run of about 25 hilly kilometres (15 miles) through exotic forest to Whangamata, headquarters for big-game fishing activity.

The road from Whangamata is a fine sealed highway, never straying far from the coast, with views from every top of the blue Pacific battering itself to pieces against white and pink cliffs topped with flaming *pohutukawa*.

The way goes through Waihi, once a mining town of some note. Gold and silver lodes were discovered in 1878 in the tree-covered area known as Martha Hill. Extensive underground workings in the ensuing seventy years fossicked out over £25,000,000 worth of precious metal. Shafts reached a depth of 1800 feet, and the total length of the drives exceeded 165 kilometres (100 miles). In one area, collapsing mines caused a subsidence which formed an extensive lake, now developed as a park. The ruins of the pumphouse which used to keep the workings as free as possible of water still stand at the entrance to the town.

Waihi is about 50 kilometres (30 miles) south of the base of the Coromandel peninsula. There is a separate settlement called Waihi Beach, situated at the northern end of an 8-kilometre (5-mile) stretch of sand and fine surf terminating at Bowentown, a tiny hamlet at the northern end of Tauranga Harbour.

Tauranga and Mount Maunganui

On the eastern edge of a gentle rolling countryside, which hides in one of its verdant valleys the Sapphire Springs, hot mineral springs organised into a small spa, is Tauranga. A small city, Tauranga curves about the southern reaches of its splendid harbour. It is growing rapidly, not least because of the fertility of the district and its rapidly expanding kiwifruit industry, kiwifruit being the grotesque name given to the fruit which used to be known as the Chinese gooseberry. The furry-coated, succulent green-fleshed fruit has won an almost addictive favour around the Pacific Basin and in various other parts of the world, with the result that a lucrative export market has grown up, and lands which were, until quite recently, used for livestock farming have been subdivided and sold off at boom prices for the establishment of kiwifruit orchards.

Tauranga is an extremely beautiful town, and one rich in historical association; for here was fought a battle which must have been the most chivalrously conducted fight of all time; and here was established and maintained Christian missionary work of the highest order and most

The Tauranga Historic Village contains original and reconstructed buildings from
the earliest days of Bay of Plenty settlement

lasting effectiveness ever recorded in this land; all of which seems,
somehow, most appropriate in this lovely Bay of Plenty.

The battle was called the Battle of Gate *Pa*. Archdeacon Brown, who
established his mission here, had the whole area fenced off to keep out
traders and others likely to corrupt his Christian converts; and when the
battle was fought, it was waged around a travesty of a *pa* which the
Maoris had constructed near the gate into the enclosure, because they did
not wish to bring the war into the mission area. The British soldiery were
less scrupulous. The area in which they camped is still called The Camp.
It is right at the tip of the Te Papa peninsula, and the area includes the
military cemetery where the dead of both sides are buried. Nearby is a fine
formal rose garden, and beyond this, a short causeway across a deep, dry
ditch which turns out, upon inspection, to be the northern rampart of the
Monmouth Redoubt. From an embrasure on its western bastion protrudes
the muzzle of a cannon. The path takes you up to the redoubt, a
surprisingly small place in which to have had a garrison plus a large
number of refugees. On its northern side, where the blockhouse once
stood, is a memorial recalling that women and children once slept there.
Armstrong guns, breech-loaders, are emplaced on the ramparts and in the
bastions, and a fat, muzzle-loading cannon, an eight or twelve pounder, is
emplaced midway along the southern rampart, with a similar six-pounder
mounted opposite, facing the gateway, as if ready to rake gate and
drawbridge with cannister. This piece, incidentally, is dated 1815, the
year of Waterloo.

Two minutes' walk from the Monmouth Redoubt – named after the
Monmouth Regiment – is the Te Papa Mission Station, including Archdeacon Brown's delightful home, The Elms, and other buildings, both
original and reconstructed. The chapel is largely a reconstruction,

housing, beside the normal furnishings of an Anglican church, well-preserved and interesting relics, including what is probably the country's finest collection of mission teaching equipment.

The lovely old house is surrounded by garden, with tall and friendly trees, brilliant flowers, and huge monarch butterflies amongst the blooms.

It is interesting to discover that amongst the deeds of heroism performed by both sides during that tragic Battle of Gate *Pa*, probably the best remembered was that of one of Brown's converts, a Maori woman named Heni te Kiri-karamu, who served with her people in Gate *Pa*. Hearing a delirious wounded soldier calling for water outside the *pa* after nightfall, she crept down to a creek, through the British lines, with a nail can, and brought it back to the thirst-tormented man. Her deed is commemorated in stained glass in Lichfield Cathedral, England, placed there by Bishop Selwyn, who was Bishop of that Diocese after his service in New Zealand.

Mount Maunganui, familiarly known to all New Zealanders simply as The Mount, is the name of a township, near enough to Tauranga to be called a suburb of that city, built upon the long spit of sand which reaches out to Maunganui (the Great Mountain) itself, where it stands forming the gatepost on the eastern side of the entrance to Tauranga Harbour. Maunganui, 232m (762ft) high, was once a Maori fortress which, according to local tradition, remained unconquered for over 100 years. That spells impregnability in anyone's language, but particularly so in the case of the Maori, who seldom took long to conquer the strongest

Above: Robbins Park lies next to Tauranga's Monmouth Redoubt
Opposite: The Elms is one of New Zealand's oldest mission buildings and
contains many relics of its builder, Archdeacon Brown

of fortresses. The earthworks are still traceable on the south-eastern side, just where you would expect to find them, since this is the landward side, from which an attack was most likely. They would have been deeper and stronger here than anywhere else on the mountain.

From the summit of Maunganui, to which well-laid but steepish paths ascend, the view is superb. You get from here a first, fascinating glimpse of White Island, which smokes 80-odd kilometres (50 miles) out to sea.

There are two islands close inshore along the ocean beach at Mount Maunganui. These are Motuotau ("Island of the Reef"), which is the farther out of the two, and Moturiki ("Small Island"), connected to the mainland by a causeway. Mount Maunganui's Marineland is built on Moturiki, constructed around a natural rock pool, and containing dolphins, sea elephants with huge, soulful eyes, New Zealand fur seals, trained sea leopards, savage creatures fully capable of killing a man, and New Zealand sea fish.

Southern Bay of Plenty

Along the coast and inland for some distance, between Tauranga and Whakatane, there is a 100-kilometre (60-mile) stretch of gently undulating country, dotted with small but prosperous settlements – Te Puke, Maketu, Pikowai, Matata and Thornton – from where a road turns inland to the billiard-table flatness of the Rangitaiki Plains. Far to the south the forested cone of Mount Edgecumbe rises above the crumpled landscape which lifts up towards the thermal area around Rotorua, and carries the

pine forests which supply the Tasman Pulp and Paper Mills of Kawerau.

Whakatane sits sandwiched between the sinuous Whakatane river on the easternmost edge of the Rangitaiki Plains, and the long, interrupted train of ridges and spurs which runs down from the Urewera Highlands. The name is said to have derived from an incident which occurred when the ancestral canoe, *Mataatua*, commanded by the mighty Toroa, landed on this spot. On reaching shore, the men immediately ran up the beach and pushed inland to see what might be seen – and, incidentally, found atop the cliffs the immense earthworks of a *pa* built by even earlier immigrants. The rising tide lifted the beached *Mataatua*, and began to float it away. The only person still on board was Toroa's patrician daughter, the beautiful Wairaka, who, seeing that the canoe was in danger, looked around desperately for the men. But none was in sight.

"I will make a man of myself, then!" she cried, and she leaped into the water, seized the huge outrigger of this big, ocean-going vessel, and somehow managed to pull the craft back on to the sand. "Whakatane" means "To act as a man".

The Strand, which is the main business area of the town, nestles beneath Puhaturoa Rock, beneath which the Bay of Plenty chiefs signed the Treaty of Waitangi. At its foot today is a canoe, a memorial to Hurunui Apanui, Chief of the Ngati-Awa, good friend of the British, beloved of *Pakeha* and Maori. The cliff itself has been sacred to the Maori for a long, long time, and is now dedicated to the dead of World War I.

The road from Whakatane to Opotiki, through the tiny village of Taneatua, runs through beautiful but rough country. Most of it is grazing land which looks as though it is uneasy in its European clothing of pasture

Above: The setting sun turns sea and sky gold at Whakatane
Opposite: The distinctive cone of the extinct volcano, Maunganui, joined to the
Bay of Plenty mainland by a sand bar on which is built the port of Mount
Maunganui

Here is a long succession of superb beaches: Hukuwai, where the surf is wild and wonderful; Tirohanga, beneath Tirohanga Bluff, site of an ancient Maori fortification; Omarumutu, where the Maori War Memorial Hall contains some of the finest existing examples of the rich, ornate East Coast style of carving; Torere, with its richly decorated Maori church and its semi-circular sweep of beach; Hawai; Maraenui Hill, 201m (660ft) high, offering a remarkable panoramic view of the bay and the whole of this East Cape coast; Maraenui Beach, where the Motu river flows strongly out into the bay; Whitianga (another one); Omaio, where the road runs along *pohutukawa*-fringed cliffs and there is a fine, steeply shelving, sheltered little bay; Little Awanui; Te Kaha, with its fine little hotel; Maungaroa ("The Long Mountain", very well named); Waikawa; Whanarua Bay; Te Waiti; Raukokore where there was once a whaling station and where trypots may still be seen rusting on the shore; Waihau Bay; and Whangaparaoa, all exquisitely beautiful coves and indentations, backed by high mountains.

The Bay of Plenty terminates at a cocked thumb of a headland, concerning which Captain Cook wrote in his log: "At 9, five canoes came off to us, in one of which there were upwards of 40 men all arm'd with Pikes, etc; from this and other Circumstances it fully appear'd that they came with no friendly intentions; and I at this time being very buisey (sic), and had no intention to stay upon the deck to watch their Motions, I order'd a Grape shot to be fir'd a little wide of them. This made them pull off a little . . . . I order'd a round shott to be fir'd over their heads, which frightened them to the degree that I believe they did not think themselves safe until they had got ashore . . . ." And as the Maoris beached their canoes and stood glowering beneath the earliest *pohutukawa* blossoms, Captain Cook, concluding his log entry, wrote: "This occasion'd our calling the Point of Land . . . Cape Runaway.".

Opposite: White Island, eternally steaming and smouldering 50 kilometres (30 miles) off the Bay of Plenty coast, provides an unforgettable sight from the air
Below: The East Cape Road, running for 340 kilometres (212 miles) between Opotiki and Gisborne, offers many views like this one of New Zealand's most easterly point

Reflections in the water at Te Puia, on the East Cape Road south of Hicks Bay, where there are hot mineral springs

The East Coast and
the Urewera

Above: The glorious scarlet flower of the *pohutukawa* blooms at Christmas
Opposite: Captain Cook, whose monument gazes out over Gisborne, first set foot on New Zealand soil at what is now the city's Kaiti Beach on 8 October 1769

The Maoris' precipitate and entirely understandable retreat from Captain Cook's whiff of grapeshot was a foretaste of what was to come. As he sailed down the eastern side of East Cape, he called into a deep, beautiful, almost landlocked bay, where he landed and approached the local Maoris with a request for food, wood and water. They allowed him wood and water only, so he called the place Poverty Bay, which it most assuredly is not.

The road which runs down the long, eastern side of the Cape is not so spectacular as that on the Bay of Plenty side, for it runs inland for much of its length, climbing, turning and twisting over ridges and through valleys. The sea is hidden by the high ranges of rugged, bush-patched hills. Yet here and there it wanders back to the coast, climbing over bluffs and broad-shouldered headlands and spurs, the toes of the Raukumara Range, and the glimpses it does afford of the sea are scenes of breathtaking beauty.

Te Araroa is one such place. Te Araroa beach, on the west bank of the Awatere river, is a long, lovely sweep of golden sand. The township nestles at the foot of a scarred limestone hill called Whatumatarau, which sprawls along the coastline like an immense, sleeping beast. Its summit was once fortified. Along this bay are *pohutukawa* trees said to have been planted by Maoris who arrived long before the so-called Great Fleet migration in the 1300s. This may be so, though there are legends and traditions which suggest that the Maoris had never seen *pohutukawa* trees before they arrived in New Zealand. Indeed, there is a proverb which runs:

"*E hoa, rukea atu to kura. Ka nui kei uta a ngangahu mai nei!*"

("Oh, friend, throw away your red feather head-dress. There are many red plumes dancing on the shore!").

This refers to a story that new arrivals, seeing *pohutukawa* blossoms bright and red in the sun, threw away the prized but faded red plumes

they had brought from their tropical homeland and rushed up the beach to pluck these new plumes, only to discover that the *pohutukawa* blossoms quickly withered. The saying is the Maori equivalent of "All is not gold that glisters".

One of the Te Araroa *pohutukawas*, an immense, spreading leviathan of a tree, is held to be the oldest, and is certainly one of the biggest, in New Zealand.

At Te Puia, almost half way down the eastern side of the Cape and fairly well inland, are hot springs containing iodides, with enough free iodine to colour the water slightly. The waters have been compared with, but are stronger than, those of Kreuznach Spa in Europe. Emissions of sulphuretted hydrogen issuing from the springs and from cracks in nearby rocks have been used occasionally for domestic lighting and heating. Spa facilities are at present being upgraded, and the spa deserves to be better known.

The road returns to the coast at Tokomaru Bay, named after one of the ancestral canoes, a pretty, seaside settlement, once a whaling station. Farther south is Tolaga Bay, where the small town stands on the bank of the Uawa river, which is navigable for shallow-draught vessels. The name, Tolaga, is probably a corruption of Tarakihi, which can either be a fish or a cicada, both of which are plentiful in this lovely bay, with its projecting, protecting headlands.

From Tolaga Bay southward the hills become increasingly tame, ridged with sheep tracks; and suddenly the road drops downward to Gisborne, a small city built mainly on the river flats about the Waimata and Taruheru rivers at the point where they join to form the Turanganui river – so close to the sea that the stretch of river from the confluence to the bay is hardly worth a name of its own. But it is wide and deep and navigable, 5m (16ft) deep at the wharves at low tide, so that ships of up to 3200 tons can berth there.

WHALING TRY POTS

Above: This lighthouse, now a memorable feature of Wairoa's Marine Parade,
once stood on Portland Island at the northern end of Hawke Bay
Opposite: Beautiful Lake Waikaremoana and Panekiri Bluff which rises a
dominating 650m (2000ft) above the lake's southern end

The bay along which much of Gisborne lies is bounded on its
southern side by a headland named Young Nick's Head, a name bestowed
by Captain Cook, who had offered a prize of a gallon of rum to the first of
his crew to see land, and two gallons if the first sighting was made by
night. The sighting was made by Nicholas Young, surgeon's boy on HMS
Endeavour. Since the lad was only twelve years old, one wonders just
what he did with his gallon of thick, potent Navy rum.

Gisborne was originally called by the Maori name for the locality,
Turanga; but this was changed for fear of confusion with Tauranga. The
name "Gisborne" is that of the Hon. William Gisborne, Colonial Sec-
retary in 1870, when the town was first surveyed.

The tall lookout hill beside the harbour is known as Kaiti Hill,
possibly because Cook chopped down the heads of some of the cabbage
trees, primitive trees whose foliage is rather like clumps of flax growing
out of the branch-ends. He had discovered the tree at Tolaga Bay, and
found that the hearts of those clumps were tender and, when boiled,
tasted not unlike cabbage. The Maori name for the tree was Ti. It is
unlikely that Cook himself named the hill, since he knew few words of
Maori, and what he did know he rendered unintelligible with his heavy
Yorkshire burr and the highly individualistic spelling of his day. He would
most likely have called it Cabbage Hill and been done with it.

The steamer *Star of Canada* went aground on Kaiti Beach in 1912,
and was totally wrecked. An enterprising citizen salvaged the entire bridge
deck and set it up ashore as a private residence, still to be seen at the

corner of Childers Road and Cobden Street, a few minutes' walk from the centre of town.

Gisborne has a fine museum containing interesting exhibits from its turbulent colonial past, a fine Maori meeting house and a number of interesting pioneer buildings in the town and around the district.

Wairoa and Lake Waikaremoana

From Gisborne, the road that goes south to Hawke's Bay begins its run across Poverty Bay Flats, where some of the country's best wines are grown. Soon, however, it begins to climb into a rugged countryside which held Gisborne in comparative isolation for many years. Roads were pushed through from the south quite early, but they were fine-weather roads, and the only practical alternative mode of transport was ship. The railway did not achieve a through service until 1942, for reasons that become apparent as you drive over the now quite splendid road from Gisborne to Wairoa. Rugged hills and wide, deep valleys and canyons posed some pretty engineering problems which, before the days of bulldozers and heavy earth-moving machinery, were all but insurmountable. Small wonder that Gisborne became the terminus for one of the country's first airlines, or that Gisborne people were well on their way to becoming seasoned air travellers by the mid-1930s.

Wairoa, on a small, flat, highly fertile river flat at the foot of the Urewera Highlands, used to be a port of some significance. The name means "Long Water", the river being navigable for shallow-draught vessels

The *kaka* is a native parrot now confined to the larger native forests of both islands. In flight, its red underwing colouring may be clearly seen

for about 20 kilometres (12 miles). Regular passenger and freight services used to operate between the Wairoa wharves and the port of Napier, to the south across the broad scoop of Hawke Bay. (Oddly, the name of the bay is Hawke Bay, whereas the name of the province is Hawke's Bay.) Wairoa is no longer important as a port, and its earliest industry, flax milling, has long since ceased. It is now just a typical small country town, though it has one link with a great metropolis. The interesting grey stone church of St Paul, modern without losing the dignity of the Gothic style, has as its foundation stone a stone from St Paul's Cathedral, London.

The road which climbs into the Urewera from Wairoa is a fitting entrance to that mysterious region. The Urewera is inhabited mainly by the Tuhoe people, known as the Children of the Mist. The story is told of how the beautiful Hine-Pokuhu-Rangi, the Mist Maid, married the mountain Maungapohatu, their offspring being the very first *tangata-whenua*, the People of the Land; which is a poetic way of saying that the true origins of the Tuhoe are lost in the mists of an olden time.

Today, the greater part of the Urewera country, 207,462 ha (455,073 acres) of rocky crags, wreathing mists and dense forest, is a National Park. Its people, the Tuhoe, live there still, in tiny, bush-bounded hamlets and steep and ferny farms. They are true highlanders, intensely clannish, apt to be a little dour, a little suspicious of lowlanders' fat and easy ways, yet containing within the highlander's crusty exterior a warm, generous, embarrassingly hospitable spirit.

The central attraction of the great park is Lake Waikaremoana, "The Sea of Rippling Waters". If you drive up to it from Wairoa on a cloudy day, or, as can often happen, a day when the rest of the world sparkles beneath a warm sun but the Urewera hides its head in the high mists, you might experience some of the awe which used to grip the old-time Maoris in the surrounding lowlands as they squatted before their fires in their bird-hunting or fishing camps and wondered what sorcery or general devilment was going on up there on those dark, fairy-haunted heights.

In the days of the Hauhau rebellion, the Armed Constabulary penetrated that then roadless wilderness, travelling up rivers in deep,

The Aniwaniwa Falls are in a beautiful bush setting a short walk from the
Urewera National Park headquarters on Lake Waikaremoana

shadowed valleys. Today, one travels comfortably up from Wairoa over a
road which is paved for some distance, but presently turns to gravelled but
well-graded surfaces. It climbs and dips around spurs and snakes along
river flats where a precious few hundred metres width of green grass and
gentle willows are grazed over by sheep and dairy cattle, hemmed in by
dense forest which climbs up into the clouds.

As the road begins to climb in earnest, the farms are left behind, and
there is nothing but many miles of primeval forest. Ancient *rimu* and *rata*
trees rear up from the tangled undergrowth. *Matai* and *totara* clothe the
ridges, and in the gullies, beside leaping, foaming mountain streams,
dense thickets of fuchsia, *mahoe* and other hardwood shrubs are splashed
with the starred tops of giant tree ferns. Sometimes you get a glimpse
from the road of a silvery ribbon of river running far below, on the floor
of a jungle-surrounded valley; and then, with a little imagination, you can
people its gravelly bed with the small, dark figures of an Armed Constabulary patrol moving very carefully upstream, alert for signals from the
Maori scouts probing ahead of them. And then, in fancy, you might hear
the weird call of conch-shell war trumpets as the wild Tuhoe tribesmen

watch, and signal the enemy's progress from mist-wreathed heights.

This is enchanted country indeed. The Tuhoe – and their ancient forebears – peopled its clearings and glades with fairies and the spirits of their ancestors. Even the trees are the People of Tane, God of the Forests, and each has a spirit. Here lives the *kaka*, that big parrot with its brownish hues, grey forehead and scarlet collar; and here also lives *ruru* the owl, also known as the Morepork, because that is what he seems to be saying when he calls across the dark valleys and black ridges soon after dusk. Bellbirds, riflemen, fantails, tomtits and most of the other small, flitting natives abound here. The bold wood pigeon sometimes clatters across the roads on heavy wings, and the *tui* flutters his white throat feathers in song too high for the human ear to hear, except for the odd bell-like note. There are wild pigs in the forest, mainly on the marginal grass and fern slopes. Goat may occasionally be seen near the road, and sambar, Japanese deer, Javan Rusa and red deer live here, though not so plentifully since shooters came in with helicopters and semi-automatic rifles and slaughtered them for the money the venison would bring.

As the road climbs higher, wisps and scarves of mist trail across it and spill down the slopes, sometimes filling the valleys with a silvery sea of cloud. Dark ridges stretch away in all directions, as far as the eye can see.

The first human habitation you reach is Tuai, a settlement established at the foot of the great, centuries-old rockfall which dammed the rivers, caused the valleys to fill, and formed Lake Waikaremoana. Water is siphoned off from the lake to produce electricity, the electricity workers living at Tuai, where you may also see your first Tuhoe people, descendants of those ancient warriors of proud and lofty lineage. Some of the older women will almost certainly have *moko* patterns – finely tattooed blue scrolls – on their lower lips and chins. It was a practice which had almost died out, but has been revived in modern times, though it is no longer done by a *tohunga* with bone chisels, but by a tattooist in Rotorua, who works to a supplied design with his electric needles. Still, it is a badge of honour and a mark of prestige.

From Tuai, the road climbs over the crest of the ridge formed by the rockfall, whose boulders may be glimpsed, huge, house-sized blocks, amongst the forest trees and vines. To the left, the Panekiri Range rises up, with peaks over 1066m (3500ft) high. On the right, reaching up to similar altitudes, are the Ngamoko ranges; and before you, gloriously blue or shining silver according to the state of the sky, lies the lovely Lake Waikaremoana.

The Lake House sits on a knoll overlooking a beautiful arm of the lake known as Te Whanganuiparua Inlet, and offers magnificent panoramic views of the lake from its pleasant lawns. Below, on the lake shore, is the motor camp, a place of green lawns stretching down to the lake from the edge of the forest.

Duck congregate here – *Putangitangi*, the paradise duck; *kuruwhengi*, the Shoveller; *papango*, the black teal ("Pango" being the Maori word for black); and *whio*, the blue duck, named for his whistling cry.

Launch trips on the lake are something of an odyssey, sailing past delightful, forest-framed beaches of white pumice sand. The Sea of Rippling Waters is transformed by a Midas Touch of the sun into an immense basin of burnished gold. The sights and vistas are memorable, including the Waiherere Bluff and the Straits of Manaia and Wairaumoana, the part of the lake once dotted with islets, perhaps before the blocked rivers had back-flooded sufficiently to cover the ridges which once separated them. Now there are just four islands. On the lake's southern shore are the towering Panekiri Cliffs, interestingly stratified and revealing to close inspection fossils of prehistoric marine life.

In the vicinity is a group of cascades known as Aniwaniwa Falls, a name (which is actually that of the river itself) meaning "Rainbow".

Willow-fringed Lake Tutira, north of Napier, is a bird-sanctuary

There is a four-day walk, complete with sleeping huts, around the lake shore – a memorable experience.

Hawke's Bay and the Wairarapa

The road south from Wairoa swings and crawls around high hills and across great ravines, through Mohaka, with its great railway viaduct, and Tutira, whose little lake is a sanctuary for wildfowl, coming down to the coast about 26 kilometres (16 miles) north of Napier, chief city of Hawke's Bay. Napier, named after one of Britain's India heroes, is not usually listed amongst New Zealand's premier resorts; perhaps it should be. Delightfully situated and with a relatively small population, it offers more in the way of amenities and assorted scenery than many a larger city, yet preserves a spaciousness and the friendly, easy-going pace of a country

Bluff Hill, round which Napier is built, once had its feet in the sea: this aerial photograph clearly shows the surrounding land uplifted by the 1931 earthquake

town. This spaciousness and Napier's curiously modern appearance often give first-time visitors the impression that the town is no more than thirty or forty years old, which is true, in a sense, though it had its beginnings in the present-day suburban area of Onepoto Gully, in 1844.

The original settlement spread inland and around the coast; by the early twentieth century it was a substantial, somewhat crowded town, with tall brick and concrete commercial buildings towering over narrow streets crowded with pedestrians and tramcars, and beginning to be even more crowded with motorcars. Then, on 3 February 1931, on a golden summer's day of cloudless skies and breathless heat, when the town was abustle and the bay a sparkling blue beneath a hot sun, disaster struck. Without warning, the ground heaved and rolled and moved in almost fluid waves, throwing down shops, office blocks, cathedral, hospital and houses. The Bluff Hill collapsed, burying vehicles on the road beneath. Power lines fell sparking as gas mains ruptured, and fires swept through the stricken city. The broad Inner Harbour west of the city disappeared in a welter of foam and fury as the bottom heaved up. Sailors on ships out in the bay watched in helpless horror as Napier was torn apart.

The ground moved, on and off, for days; but after the first, biggest shocks, Napier people, those who survived, rolled up their sleeves, first throwing up what was known as "Tin Town" in Clive Square; then they built a new, better city. Previously unable to expand outward because of swamps on their southern side, they now found themselves able to build outward almost without restriction. Understandably, they avoided multi-storey building, though tall buildings have been built over the past twenty years; even today, chimneys of houses throughout Central Hawke's Bay tend to be stubby, barely above roof-level.

90

This statue of Pania of the Reef, a maiden in a Maori legend of the Sea People,
is set on Marine Parade in Napier

The Marine Parade grew into a glorious area of garden, restaurant,
aquarium, Sound Shell and other amenities, built over rubble from the
old city. The Norfolk pines, which have been there since before the
'quake, are nowadays festooned with lights, like huge Christmas trees.
And at one point there is the Colonnade, glazed so that you can sit
sheltered from the wind, overlooking the sea; inside hangs the bell from
HMS *Veronica*, a Navy sloop which was in harbour at the time of the
earthquake, and whose crew rendered invaluable assistance. There is also
the statue of Pania of the Reef, that sweet-faced Maori maid whose story
is remarkably like that of Hans Andersen's Little Mermaid at Copenhagen, and who sits gracefully on her rock.

The Napier Museum is a particularly fine one, noted for its collection
of Maori artifacts, and for its collection of photographs of early Napier,
and of Napier just before, during and immediately after the earthquake.
The Waiapu Cathedral, "this huge and lovely Cathedral", the Archbishop
of Canterbury called it at a dedication service in 1965, has, like Napier
itself, risen on the ruins of an earlier building. (The first donations
towards the new cathedral came from three English children who, the
Diocese remembers with affection, sent five shillings each of their holiday
pocket money.)

The Hawke's Bay and Wairarapa coastline, unlike the ragged coast
north of Gisborne, sweeps southward in a long, almost unbroken series of
sandy bays interspersed with short, stubby headlands and backed by high
hills and cliffs. The southern extremity of Hawke Bay is Cape Kidnappers,
so named because the Maoris hereabouts tried to kidnap the Tahitian lad
whom Captain Cook had brought with him as an interpreter.

At its extreme end is the world-famous gannet colony, near the

The tip of Cape Kidnappers is thought to be one of the few mainland places in the world where gannets have formed a breeding colony

extreme tip of the cape, which runs down from its lighthouse in a series of long swoops, rather like the tail of a dragon, formidably spiked. The final joint of the tail is beneath the sea, but the last spike still pokes up out of the angry, broken water. The second-to-last joint of the "tail" is the site of the great nesting ground. It is a shallow bowl of bare, rocky ground, leaning to the sun and dotted during the nesting season, between November and February, with thousands of gannet pairs and their chicks. There is another gannetry a few hundred metres south-west of the cape. This is on a flat plateau about 110m (360ft) above the sea, and is much easier to reach than the larger gannetry on the Cape Kidnappers itself, though the cape gannetry provides a more spectacular sight, since visitors are taken by the Ranger, a few at a time, amongst the thousands of snowy-white birds. But the path is dangerous for those without a good head for heights, leading as it does along precipitous slopes and down steep, razor-backed ridges.

The gannet seen in these colonies is the Australian gannet, *Sula serrator*, whose normal nesting places are small, rocky islets off the coast. It is extemely rare to find them nesting on the mainland. They are relatives of the pelican and the shag, sharing the pelican's ungainliness on land, but surpassing him in grace and beauty on the wing, as much a master of their element as the albatross.

Inland from the coast, Hastings, sister-city to Napier and, like Napier, named for a British leader in India, sits on the Heretaunga Plain, one of the fruit bowls of New Zealand. From its southern edge, the land rises up, not dramatically but gently, to become a smiling, green, rolling country of sheep farms, small patches of bush and gentle rivers. Such is its nature all the way south to the bottom edge of the North Island; and the rolling, smooth, cultivated character of the hills scarcely changes even where they rise up to become the foothills of the Ruahine and Tararua ranges.

Fifty kilometres (30-odd miles) south of Hastings, the Takapau Plain spreads out on either side of the Tukituki river, little more than a broad river valley, and then the hills close in again. Little villages nestle

92

Springtime in the beautiful Queen Elizabeth Park in Masterton

amongst the valleys in a vast area of country which was once *totara* forest, but was cleared, and the timber milled, by Scandinavian immigrants whose descendants still live hereabouts, on rare occasions keeping Norse festivals and appearing in Danish or Norwegian national costume. Their villages, towns and various country localities have evocative names, like Norsewood, and, third largest Hawke's Bay town, Dannevirke.

At Norsewood is an excellent little colonial museum, the Scandy House, in which the Scandinavians' way of life has been preserved. Painted a distinctive barn red with white facings, the attractive little house is a veritable time machine. Seeing the kitchen, for example, one half expects a practical housewife to be bustling about, setting bread in the colonial oven, hand-grinding coffee, or pouring it, a steaming fragrant brew, from the enamelled coffee pot with the wooden handle sticking out from its side. The illusion is heightened by the fact that from time to time local ladies actually do bake in that kitchen, so that it has a cooked-in smell. The parlour and the bedrooms are real rooms, with everything that went to make the difference between shanty living and a well-organised, tasteful nineteenth-century home. In the parlour, Father's meerschaum pipe, a twist of black shag tobacco, and shredding and cutting implements still lie on an occasional table beside his sacrosanct chair, and the children's blocks are still scattered on the floor, where they left them at bedtime. In the bedroom, a colourful Danish text hangs on the wall over the bed with its exquisite knitted string bedspread, and a clean, white nightshirt spread on it. There's a watch-stand on Father's side of the bed, and a Bible shelf on Mother's, with a night-light.

South of Hawke's Bay, through the Wairarapa, the country tends to become a little steeper, a little rougher, in towards the Tararua Range.

The Castlepoint lighthouse on the Wairarapa coast is one of the tallest in the country and of some importance on a coast which can be treacherous

The main road goes through towns with musical names – Mangatainoka, Pahiatua, Eketahuna (once named Mellemskov by the Scandinavians who settled there when it was a forest fastness) – and slips in between the bird sanctuary of Mount Bruce and the now close-by Tararuas. Masterton, chief town of the Wairarapa, is well laid-out, with fine parks and reserves, notably Queen Elizabeth Park which has aviaries, an aquarium and a boating lake.

North-eastwards from Masterton, where a good road runs through the hilly Maungaraki Range, is Castlepoint. Kupe, the Polynesian navigator, discovered the rocky headland about AD 925, when he was reputedly searching for a great octopus which had become a danger to life and limb along that coast; he found it, so legend says, in a cave under the rock on which the Castlepoint lighthouse now stands. It was probably from the very fine beach at Castlepoint that he pushed inland and explored the Wairarapa. It is a superb beach, where the great Pacific rollers come surging in, to rear up, curl under and break on the reef which stretches south from the point. The point itself, a rocky headland thrusting out from the southern end of the beach, is connected to the mainland by a low causeway of rock and clay, to which clings stubborn, salt-burnt grass. The lighthouse stands out on the tip, white against the sky.

Castlepoint was named by Captain Cook, who likened its towering rock to a castle. Since Cook's time, however, successive earthquakes and storms have whittled away, ground down and tumbled the castle's ramparts, and the resemblance is now slight indeed.

South of Masterton, Carterton is the jumping-off place for Mount

The "Cobblestones" stable at Greytown was built in the mid-1850s and used by the famous Cobb and Co. coaches; today it is a museum

Holdsworth, 23 kilometres (14 miles) north-westward, in the Tararua range, where there is a good skifield in season. The mountain is 1336.5m (4385ft) high, with a mountain hut about half way up.

From Carterton, the road winds on down to Greytown, the oldest town in the Wairarapa, founded in 1854 and named in honour of Sir George Grey. It is a charming village, surrounded by orchards; here, in 1881, was founded the first co-operative dairy factory in Australasia – that is, a dairy factory run by and for farmers, to take their cream and manufacture butter. The district is also noted for a small *pa* at Papawai, once a centre of Maori culture, a conscious attempt by Maori leaders to revive a race which, after the wars of the 1860s, was tending to turn its face to the wall. It is unique in one particular. The carved human figures on the palisades were made to face inwards, as they do today. The palisades are gone, but the posts with the carved figures remain. Usually, such figures faced outward, grimacing horribly to deter attackers. But at Papawai, their leader, old Tamahau Mahupuku declared to his dispirited people "The only enemies of our people are *inside* the *pa*, today".

There is a flat, meandering road from Papawai and Greytown to Martinborough, a town created by a local landowner, Sir John Martin, to service the farming community, and laid out by him to commemorate a world tour, and to express his pride in all things British. The streets in the centre of the town form the Union Jack.

From Martinborough the road drifts like an amiable inebriate, weaving its way down past Lake Ferry, to the wild Palliser Bay coast, which looks out across Cook Strait at the South Island.

Warbrick Terrace in the Waimangu thermal valley gets its colours from the effects of varying temperatures on the hot water algae present. In this valley were the Pink and White Terraces destroyed by the Mount Tarawera eruption in 1886

The Thermal Area and the
Central Volcanic Plateau

Rotorua, Buried Village and the Thermal Lakes

About 50 kilometres (30 miles) inland from the central Bay of Plenty coast is Rotorua. The name means "Two Lakes" or "Second Lake" and is said to derive from the fact that the *Arawa* canoe chief, Ihenga, discovered Lake Rotorua after first stumbling upon Lake Rotoiti. He named the second lake after his uncle and father-in-law, Kahu-mata-momoe. He called it Rotorua-nui-a-Kahu, *roto* meaning "lake", *rua* meaning "second", *nui* meaning "large". Some doubt attaches to this story, however, since on arrival Ihenga discovered a chief named Tua-roto-rua already there, and the lake could well have been named after him. But there is another meaning which may well be ascribed to the lake, and one which makes good sense. Rotorua can be translated as "Lake of the Pit", and in view of the fact that it occupies a depression caused by volcanic activity, and because of the nature of its surroundings, this translation is likely to be the correct one.

Rotorua city is fairly large, with a population of about 50,000 people. It sits on the shore of Lake Rotorua, which itself is the principal lake in a group of waters which are all of direct or indirect volcanic origin. It is a roughly pear-shaped water 83 square kilometres (32 square miles) in area, which drains some 413 square kilometres (159 square miles) of country, and which flows out into its smaller near-neighbour, Rotoiti, which means, naturally enough, "Small Lake".

Rotorua is the home of the great Arawa federation of tribes, a fighting people who have long been good friends of the *Pakeha*, and Lake Rotorua is especially identified with them. Mokoia Island, in the eastern half of the lake, was the southern limit of the musket-supported depredations of the Ngapuhi chieftain, Hongi Ika, who defeated the Arawa there, but received such a mauling in the process that he had to retreat. It is also the scene of the Maoris' classic love story, the tale of Hinemoa, who swam out to the island to be united with her lover, Tutanekai, overcoming a parental ban. Hinemoa's Pool, a hot pool cut into the rock of the island, is still there.

There is a road running around the shores of Lake Rotorua, along which are many beauty spots and scenic attractions, including the thermal area of Tikitere, sometimes called Hell's Gate, a frankly weird place of petrified tree roots, boiling cauldrons, sulphurous atmosphere and subterranean rumblings, where the solid rock trembles underfoot with the vigour of these infernal boilings. Rotokawau, "The Lake of the Shag", is in this vicinity, a forest-set gem of a lake in the crater of an ancient volcano. Rotoiti is also close by, comparable with Waikaremoana in its wealth of wooded islets, its forest-crowned bluffs pierced high up by burial caves, and the sloping *maraes* of Maori villages and their terraced gardens.

Okere Falls, not far from the Ohau Channel between Rotoiti and Rotorua, are rather lovely, falling into a wooded dell where the white water foams into a deep green pool in the Kaituna ("Feast of Eels") river.

In the area as well are the Hamurana Springs amongst encircling poplar and California redwood trees, with a deer park; and the Taniwha and Rainbow Springs, where the water is miraculously clear, and full of fat trout and mallard ducks. Yet another such place, perhaps the pick of them all, is called Fairy Springs and often, with reason, the Gem of the World. Here, the Maoris claim quite seriously, the Little People, the Patu-paiarehe, lived as recently as 500 years ago. Here welling springs carry up silent fountains of white pumice and black grains of obsidian, saturating the calm waters with it, lending them the loveliest shades of blue. You can hold out food a metre above the water, and watch as fat rainbow trout rocket up out of a milling, iridescent shoal of their fellows, leap through the air at lightning speed and take it from your fingers.

Trout, among them the largest captive specimens in the world, are fed by hand
in the five trout pools at Rainbow Springs near Rotorua

Above: A Maori Christ seems to be walking across the waters of Lake Rotorua,
seen through this window in St Faith's Anglican Church, Ohinemutu
Opposite: The Maori lovers Hinemoa and Tutanekei embrace over the gateway
to the model *pa* and Maori Arts and Crafts Reserve at Whakarewarewa

On the northern side of Rotorua is Ohinemutu, variously translated,
but probably meaning "The Place of the Youngest Daughter". Ohinemutu
is a community within a community, a Maori microcosm in a *Pakeha*
macrocosm. Here Maoris live, work, worship and, eventually, die and are
buried. The "village square" is a flat, tar-sealed rectangle of ground
surrounded by houses, most of which are European in style. But the great
whare-runanga which presides over this *marae* is one of the finest examples
of the carvers' skill still in general use; and the interior of the lovely
Church of St Faith, on the lake shore, is rich in intricate carvings and
fine *tukutuku* panels, and a famous window depicting a Maori Christ, so
placed that from within the church he appears to be walking towards you
on the waters of the lake.

At Ohinemutu is a notable carving centre. The Arawa have produced
long lines of outstanding carvers, and Arawa work has always been highly
prized. In this centre, it is possible to watch the carvers as they work —
mostly on souvenirs nowadays. But they are good souvenirs, a safer
purchase than from many a souvenir shop. The centre displays fake Maori
carving, mainly produced in the Pacific islands and commonly sold as
genuine Maori work.

Rotorua's most famous attraction is Whakarewarewa, sometimes translated as "The Place of Rising Steam". It is, of course, New Zealand's best-
known thermal area. The two sides of the Whakarewarewa valley are
virtually separate entities, with the western side, known as the Maori Arts
and Crafts Reserve, entered by way of a model *pa*, which is not a real
fighting *pa* but is a fair enough representation of a lightly fortified village.

Its gateway carries a carved representation of Hinemoa and Tutanekai embracing, and within is a fine collection of carved *pataka* (food store-houses), carved *whare-puni* (sleeping houses), and less ornate sleeping houses. There is also a canoe, upended in a shady corner of the *pa*, as a monument to a dead chief.

In the valley beneath the *pa*, and across on the other side, are the pools of boiling mud, a rather weird lake known as Rotowhio, fumaroles which hiss and roar and grumble enthusiastically and sometimes a little alarmingly, like the bursting pipes of some infernal boiler room, silica terraces and, on the crest of a frozen wave of alum, the world-famous Pohutu Geyser and its companion, the equally famed Prince of Wales Feathers, a triple jet which usually precedes the playing of Pohutu.

The other entrance to the valley is through the Maori Thermal Reserve, with its modern Maori village, whose children dive from the entrance bridge for coins tossed into the river, and where *wahines* (girls) may sometimes be seen cooking the family vegetables in a flax kit lowered into a boiling pool.

The Government Gardens at the city centre were for years a spa, and the mock-Tudor bathhouse is still used as a restaurant and civic centre. The spa still exists, but has been modernised and upgraded.

South-east of Rotorua are the Blue and Green Lakes, and Lake Tarawera. Blue Lake is a wonderful lapis lazuli sort of blue, regardless of whether blue sky or grey overcast prevails. Its Maori name is Tikitapu, "Sacred Being", and the lake is said to be inhabited by a *taniwha*, a sort of water-dragon, though the monster might not be the sacred being to whom

Pohutu geyser often gushes an impressive 30m (100ft) into the air at
Whakarewarewa

The Wairakei geothermal project, where more than 100 bores have been sunk,
contributes significantly to New Zealand's electricity supply

The Rainbow Terrace and Hochstetter Cauldron at the Geyserland thermal area,
Orakei Korako, north of Taupo

The Huka Falls, on the Waikato River, descend 11m (35ft) into a deep basin
after rushing awesomely through a narrow chasm

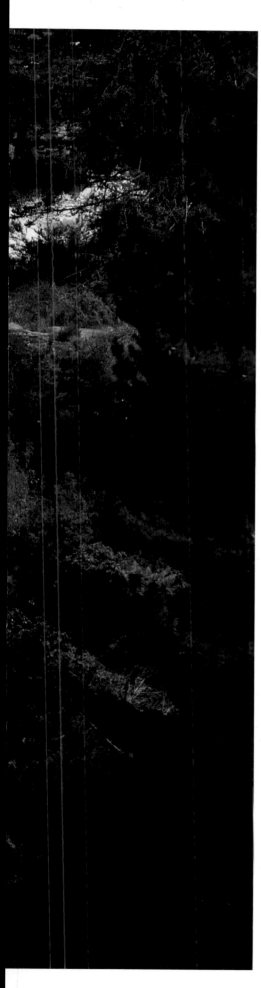

Orakei Korako lies 33 kilometres (21 miles) north of Taupo. For many years its once considerable thermal activity diminished until, in 1961, a hydro-electric dam was erected on the Waikato, and the water backed up to fill its valley and form the lovely Lake Ohakuri. Almost immediately, the thermal activity at Orakei Korako seethed into new life. It is among the most beautiful and fascinating of all the thermal areas, where the Diamond Geyser scatters jewels of water with a prodigal hand, letting them spill carelessly down her coral pink silica skirts. Hochstetter Cauldron hurls forth 4,500,000 litres of boiling water a day in explosive pulses of energy. The Rainbow Terrace and the Coronation Robes display their delightful draperies, Aladdin's Cave is colourful with its emerald green pool and brightly coloured walls, the fabulous Golden Fleece dips its edge into the Lady Cobham Geyser, and the famous Artist's Palette is a flat expanse of silica splodged with coloured pools of steaming water. The whole area is in a stage setting of green fronds of tall *ponga* tree ferns.

A little distance upstream from the Wairakei Project are the Huka Falls, where the Waikato river rushes insanely between confining rock walls, to leap, roaring, over a rock ledge into a maelstrom which quickly calms and becomes a broad, green stretch of water of startling clarity. The rapids are crossed by a strong, firm suspension bridge, beyond which is a steel-railing fence all the way to a vantage point from which the best views and photographs may be obtained. This is not a particularly high fall, but is one of New Zealand's most spectacular, a terrifying stretch of brutally powerful water.

Downstream, the Falls have a companion, the Aratiatia Rapids. When the New Zealand Electricity Department built a dam across the Waikato just above this point, there was an immediate – and justified – outcry that one of the country's most awe-inspiring sights was about to be destroyed. Fortunately, the engineers and the Department displayed commendable concern and considerable imagination; for they did not merely preserve, but actually improved the spectacle. The dam has huge floodgates, which are opened twice a day. A warning siren sounds as they open, and the water comes foaming and jetting forth. The narrow, rocky ravine is lying, at one moment, peacefully still, a barely connected chain of pools and runlets. Within five minutes, it fills to become a roaring, frenzied, appalling flood, crashing and pounding its way down that twisted passage to the trembling of the very ground beneath your feet and a cacophony of water-sound that startles the hitherto still valley.

Te Porere and Tongariro National Park

The rebel Te Kooti forced a chieftain, Te Heuheu Horonuku, and his followers, to be his unwilling allies in the struggle against the Government. Te Heuheu gave the Hauhau rebels minimal assistance which stopped short of actual fighting; but this was sufficient to cause several opportunists amongst the friendly Maoris who had fought for the government to ask for Te Heuheu's territory as a reward for their loyal service. Te Heuheu forestalled them by offering the three mountains on the central volcanic plateau to the nation, for use as a national park. The volcanoes, Ruapehu, Tongariro and Ngauruhoe, are sacred; indeed, legend had it that Te Heuheu's ancestor had had the fires in those smouldering volcanoes lit.

Te Kooti fought his last fight at a *pa* he had built on the tilted tussock country which slopes up towards the mountains. It is still there, a well-preserved earthwork fort from which he escaped and fled into forest

territory where he knew his friends would hide him.

The road from Te Porere takes a southward turn and weaves a wavering, carelessly drawn course across the tussock land which slopes gently upward to those uprearing, snow-capped volcanic peaks, now known as Ruapehu, Ngauruhoe and Tongariro; "now known" because, originally, and still more correctly, Tongariro was the name for all three.

Mount Tongariro, its broken, headless trunk rising to a height of 1968m (6458ft) above Lake Rotoaira and the more or less flat lands between that placid water and Te Porere *pa*, is an interesting area. On its southern slopes stands Okahukura Bush, a splendid expanse of forest, mainly Hall's *totara*, a tree which is virtually indistinguishable from mountain beech to the non-botanical eye. The forest is the haunt of both long-tailed and shining cuckoos in the summer months.

Flanking it is a fascinatingly weird area known as Ketetahi Springs, which is at least half a day's tramp from the road. For sheer bizarreness it has no peer, even at famous Wairakei or Rotorua. On the many-cratered slopes of Tongariro is a sight which must surely be an approximation of what the world was like when it was very young. Fumaroles hiss and burble everywhere. Small geysers incessantly hurl boiling water into the air, and breathe out clouds of sulphurous steam. Mud boils and burps and glops in porridge-pot pools, hot springs come gushing from fissures, blowholes roar deafeningly, and a heavy though not too unpleasant smell of sulphur hangs hellishly in the air.

From Ketetahi Springs, a good walking track goes to the Middle Crater of Tongariro, Te Mari Crater, on the northern face, still active in a peaceable, grumbling sort of way, with signs in its vicinity of a fairly recent lava flow.

The track runs around the edge of Middle Crater via a midget desert

Surely one of the most impressive mountain vistas in the North Island: Mounts Ruapehu, Ngauruhoe and Tongariro raise snow-clad peaks to the sky

of scoria and pumice, to Blue Lake, an exquisite gem of mineral-laden water; then past some more jewels in Tongariro's castellated crown known, unimaginatively if naturally, as the Green Lakes. Red Crater is not far from these small lakelets, steaming and smoking, its red sides streaked with bars of black and white. It is possible to go on from here, over a footwear-punishing hill of scoria and down to a track which skirts the broad, bare, flat expanse of South Crater. The path goes around the tumbled debris from Ngauruhoe, climbs up to the Mangatepopo Saddle and on to Ngauruhoe's summit, an up-and-back trip taking about six and a half hours. A slightly taxing tramp in summer, as all the approaches to the powerfully sulphurous summit of Ngauruhoe are, in winter it is a climb for competent mountaineers. And, naturally, it must be attempted only when the crater is quiescent.

The southernmost mountain of the three volcanoes, Mount Ruapehu, stands some distance from the central peak, Ngauruhoe. The Chateau, which is a very fine tourist hotel, and the village, with its small museum, its motor camp and its cabin accommodation, sit almost midway between the two peaks. Here, skiers gather during the snow season (usually between June and the end of September) to enjoy some of the country's finest snow slopes.

Aside from the skifields, Ruapehu's most famous feature is the Crater Lake, which can be reached by way of the chairlift and the tracked snow vehicle known as the Whakapapa Cat, which runs from the top of the

Above: Mount Ngauruhoe belches gas and steam into the air as ash
and lava flow down its sides during one of the mountain's periodic
eruptions
Opposite: Skiers enjoying a run on the Whakapapa side of Mount
Ruapehu, which at 2796m (9175ft) is the highest peak in the
North Island

chairlift to the summit. The lake is hot, though surrounded by ice and snow, for this mountain, also, is an active volcano. Periodically it erupts, and the lake disappears, to be replaced by smoking lava. In between times, it steams contentedly, like a giant soup cauldron. Tourist posters used to show scenes of people standing on the crater's lip in skiing gear, while others, usually shapely maidens, sat at the lake's edge in swimsuits. But it is doubtful whether anyone has actually swum in its waters, which are very acid.

Ngauruhoe's crater, by contrast, is an awesome, horrid pit.

There are many fine scenic walks around Ruapehu, featuring waterfalls, interesting plant life and panoramic views; and on a clear day, across many kilometres of bush-clad, dark green ranges, it is possible to see Mount Egmont, the North Island's other major volcanic cone, rearing up from West Cape, ghostly in the hazy distance.

A seascape characteristic of the North Island's west coast: a rock-strewn sea and a lonely shoreline edged with rugged, windswept cliffs

The North Island's West Coast and the Waikato

The great Waikato river flows peaceably through Hamilton, its banks lush with
the trees and vegetation of the parks with which the city is well endowed

If the east coast of the North Island possesses a tranquil beauty in its
sandy bays and its scenes of pastoral peace, the west coast is distinguished
by a wind-blown wildness, with great stretches of rock-bound, crashing
coastline from which the hills go back forested from the sea, ridge on
precipitous ridge, until, along the wide curve of the South Taranaki
Bight, the hills retreat far inland, and the plains and the meandering
rivers come down to a low-lying sweep of coast, an almost continuous,
magnificent beach separated from the pastoral hinterland by desert-like
stretches of dune, until, over the last 64 kilometres (40 miles) of coast,
the hills creep back, and the coastline is armoured in rocky reef, and
indented with lagoon and inlet.

The Waikato river, coming down from Lake Taupo to the western
coast, flows strongly across a rolling, inland basin. It is joined by the
much smaller Waipa river, which flows down from the Pirongia Range, to
form with the Waikato a large delta of remarkable fertility. At the
confluence of the two rivers stands the tiny town of Ngaruawahia, chosen
by the Maori king, Potatau, as his capital. Potatau's authority was denied,
and his kingship opposed by the Government of the day. A bloody war
was fought, which drove the Kingite Maoris from the Waikato-Waipa
delta, into the forests of the King Country, and a military frontier, known
as the Aukato Line, was set up. The regiments which guarded this
frontier farmed the confiscated lands, and built the thriving towns.

Today, Potatau's direct descendant, Queen Te Ata-i-rangi-kaahu, has
her Residence there, and is a deeply respected figure, possessing no
governmental power, but having a wide influence amongst the Maori
people. The "palace" is rather charming, a European house in general
design, but with beautifully carved wooden panels in place of the usual
weatherboards, and elaborately carved bargeboards and dormers.

The principal town of the Waikato is Hamilton, a pleasant city
standing astride the Waikato and rapidly developing into one of the
largest New Zealand cities. It is also a university town of note. Most of
the other Waikato towns are smallish country centres such as Cambridge,
of gentle, rather English aspect; and one-time popular resort towns like Te

114

A Maori war canoe is paddled across Lake Karapiro which was created to build
the Karapiro dam on the Waikato

Aroha, crouching beneath the Kaimai Ranges, and Matamata, which
possess notable mineral springs. Matamata still attracts visitors, who come
to bathe in its hot pools.

From Raglan Harbour, which was once a port of some importance but
has declined with the diminishing of coastal shipping, the coastline bulges
out around the forest-crowned Mount Karioi, curving down to the
landlocked harbours of Aotea and Kawhia, separated from each other by a
neck of land on which spreads the township of Kawhia, birthplace of
another famous Maori chieftain, Te Rauparaha. Kawhia is the cradle of
the Waikato people. Here, around 1350, landed the great ancestral
canoe, *Tainui*. After travelling along the east coast, touching at Opotiki,
Tauranga, Whitianga, Hauraki and Tamaki, she was portaged across the
Tamaki Isthmus and into Manukau Harbour, whence she sailed down the
west coast, landing at Mokau. Some of her crew eventually brought her
back to Kawhia, where she lies buried to this day.

In the hills inland of Kawhia, the Pakoka stream plunges over a rocky
ledge into a basin, a drop of about 49m (160ft) called the Bridal Veil
Falls. The basin is a weird place – or would be if it were not for the lacy
beauty of the falls and the brightness of the sunshine and the blue sky –
for it hints at some tremendous cataclysm in ages past, some brutal force
tearing its way up through the earth's surface, twisting the rock horren-
dously and leaving a gaping wound. Today the rock is mossy and hung
with fern. It juts out to form an overhang, shrubs grow about its feet and
trees crowd down to the water's edge, around an amazingly placid basin in
spite of that long plunge.

Kawhia is a big and beautiful harbour, capable of being developed into
a deep-water port. Its 20-kilometre (12-mile) length and 10-kilometre (6-
mile) width is fed by five streams, the estuaries of which are all navigable
by launch; the surrounding, bush-clad hills are a natural paradise of bird
life, waterfalls and caves. The township itself is very small, idyllic and
quaint with its waterfront stores and its *pohutukawa* trees, one of which
disputes with the Te Araroa *pohutukawa* the title of the greatest, most
venerable *pohutukawa* in New Zealand, it being generally agreed that if

the Te Araroa tree is the oldest, the Kawhia tree is the biggest.

There is a *marae*, a tribal meeting ground, down near the water's edge, with a big *whare-runanga* with carved bargeboards over its front porch. It is built, as are most such buildings, to catch the sun and trap it in its porch, to warm the interior and give it ample light. Not far around the beach is the resting place of the canoe *Tainui*. It is buried, as the Vikings and Saxons buried their ships, and its length, which must be close to 31m (100ft) is marked by two upright stones. This is sacred ground indeed.

There is another great canoe at Kawhia, the *waka-taua* of the chief Te Rauparaha of bloody memory, last of the great old-time chiefs, who subjugated tribes in both the North and the South Islands in the 1820s. Eventually, in the 1840s, he clashed with the British, was arrested and kept aboard a warship in Waitemata Harbour. He was born at Kawhia, and to Kawhia, after his death, they brought his war canoe. They sank it in the harbour, and the locals today can point out the stones which mark the position of its bow and stern and pick out its outline. They are visible only at low tide.

Kawhia possesses hot springs, the Te Puia Hot Springs; they are open to the sky, available simply by scooping a hole in the sand.

Waitomo Caves

From Albatross Point, the coast steps southward, swinging out in a curve to Tirua Point. Behind it, the limestone hills are tall and steep and riddled with subterranean waterways. It is a massively crumpled country-side, patched with bush but largely open farmland, forming part of the Waitomo District. "Waitomo" is a composite word, *wai* meaning "water",

---

The Bridal Veil Falls, in the hills between Raglan and Kawhia drop an impressively sheer 49m (160ft) from a rock fissure into a pool beneath

---

and *tomo* meaning "to pass in or out". *Tomo* has come to be taken locally to mean "hole", because from time to time subsidences occur, and farmers find holes opening in their paddocks. Some of the larger subsidences have opened long, deep ravines in which the rivers are open to the sky, emerging from one cave and disappearing into another. Hence the "passing in or out". The area is part of a huge limestone reef, and limestone country is almost invariably cave country.

The Waitomo Caves are, however, unique. There are three main caves in the complex. The first, called, simply, the Waitomo Cave, is on tribal lands once belonging to the Ngati-Hau tribe. They were dispossessed by the Ngati-Uekaka of Kawhia, under the chief Tane Tinorau. When Tane Tinorau's time came to die, his body was placed on a sort of overhung ledge above a second cave, called Ruakuri, which means "Den of Dogs". The ledge was marked by a smear of red ochre, and old Tane's body is still there. The third cave, Aranui, was discovered in 1911 by a Maori from the Waitomo *kainga*, who was hunting wild pig. His name was Ruruku Aranui, and it is doubly fitting that this cave should have been named after him, because "Aranui" means "Big Pathway", which describes the interior of this cavern exactly.

Waitomo Cave was first explored by a man named Fred Mace, assistant to a surveyor working on the Main Trunk Railway, with a Maori, a descendant of Tane Tinorau, also named Tane Tinorau. They examined the cave, floating down its ice-cold river on a raft, with only candles for illumination. Tane, with his wife, Hute Tane, ultimately exploited it, leading visitors up and down crude wooden ladders, lighting their way with candles and illuminating special features with magnesium

---

Looking south over Kawhia and its lovely, isolated harbour, last resting place of the canoe *Tainui* which brought the Polynesians in the 14th century

---

flares. Today, under Government control, Waitomo Cave is easy to reach and safe to explore, with competent, knowledgeable guides, electric lighting and well-formed walk-ways.

Waitomo's best-known attraction is the Glow-Worm Grotto. It is entered by way of a stairway which leads down to a jetty beside a still, black pool where, beneath a single shaded bulb, a flat-bottomed boat is tied. It is an eerie scene, wanting only a Charon to complete a picture which could well have inspired a Gustave Doré engraving. The guide whispers a cautioning "All quiet, please", and switches off the light. The boat glides out from the jetty, its motion sensed rather than felt in the unrelieved blackness.

Gradually light-starved eyes become aware of a faint glow in the solid darkness above, and faint pinpoints of light assume definite positions, one by one, and then, by tens and hundreds and thousands, whole constellations of blue-green stars appear, and the close blackness seems to enlarge and lighten until the underground river in an 80m- (50ft-) high cavern takes on the appearance of a glassy sea beneath an infinite sky. (As a matter of prosaic fact, the "glassy sea" is a backwater of the Waitomo river, and the "stars" are small, worm-like creatures known as the New Zealand Glow-Worm, *Arachnocampa luminosa*, in a colony estimated to consist of around a hundred thousand glow-worms, the larval stage of a gnat-like insect resembling, though smaller than, a daddy-long-legs. The light is used to catch food in the form of midges, and is produced by a chemical reaction within the glow-worms' bodies.

Aranui Cave has none of the vast chambers of Waitomo or Ruakuri Caves, but is a twist of comparatively narrow passages hung with fantastic almost fluid formations of recrystallised limestone.

Ruakuri is entered by way of a stairway beneath a rock overhang. The stairway terminates in a small door which opens into a blackness which, from outside, seems scarcely dispelled by the electric light which the guide switches on. Its chief glory is the Royal Court, with coruscating, bizarrely sculpted formations of breath-taking beauty massed tier upon tier.

The King Country, Northern Taranaki and New Plymouth

Between Tirua Point and the westward-thrusting coastline of West Cape, the land is prodigiously crumpled, with the hills coming down to terminate in high cliffs and steep, gully-riven littorals, with numerous streams and two sizeable, navigable rivers rushing out into the Tasman Sea. The towns are small, tucked into close valleys well inland. This is the King Country, the tract of steep, forested land into which the Maori King and his followers were not so much banished as forced to withdraw, under the protection of the Ngati-Maniapoto people. Te Kuiti is just such a town. The name is a contraction of Te Kuititanga, which means "The Narrowing-In". On the southern outskirts of the town is the great *whare-runanga*, Te Tokanganuianoho, built by the Ngati-Maniapoto people, still unreconciled to the *Pakeha*, in honour of the rebel Te Kooti, when he sought refuge in the King Country after the massacre of a detachment of troopers near Taupo.

The road through this lofty country comes down to the coast at Awakino, where the canoe *Tainui* landed and rested for some time before being returned to Kawhia and buried. The beaches hereabouts are of black ironsand, with immense rollers crashing in from the Tasman Sea, and a strong and dangerous rip. The Awakino is not a particularly big river, but

Opposite: Tens of thousands of the larvae of the remarkable *Arachnocampa luminosa*, lighten the darkness of the Glow-Worm Grotto in the Waitomo Cave

Above: Cattle enjoy good grazing in the King Country, that part of the Waikato to which the Maori King and his followers retreated in the 1860s
Opposite: Mokau Inlet, where the river was a boundary between the Taranaki and Waikato Maoris and therefore scene of numerous inter-tribal battles

a little farther down the coast is the Mokau, which is navigable for launches, and carried a heavy traffic of coastal vessels for a considerable distance upstream before it was partially blocked during the great flood of 1913. Some 40 kilometres (25 miles) upstream are the Mangapohue Rapids, and launch trips to this point pass through scenery which rivals that of the more famous Wanganui river. Mighty bluffs and dense forest on either side of the broad, deceptively calm stretches of this powerful river make it one of New Zealand's finest scenic waterways. At Mokau, the last artillery shots of the New Zealand Wars were fired in 1869, when Colonel Whitmore reconnoitered the Mokau Heads as a preliminary to carrying out a punitive expedition against marauding Maoris who had massacred a garrison at Pukearuhe, farther south. One of his troopships, the *Sturt*, fired a few shells at a *kainga* called Te Kauri, but the chief, Wetere, and his people had already fled upstream in their canoes.

From Kawhia, through Awakino and Mokau to Tongaporutu, the coastal cliffs and hillsides are clothed in a lovely shrub known as golden tainui which, according to legend, sprang from the timbers of the canoe *Tainui*. Legend also suggests that it stops at Tongaporutu because the land beyond the Tongaporutu is Tokomaru territory, being the final anchorage of the ancestral canoe *Tokomaru* in or about 1350. Science, in its prosaic, killjoy fashion, calls the shrub *Pomaderris apetala* and points out that it grows in many other localities.

At the mouth of the Tongaporutu river are great sandstone cliffs, riddled with caverns; and just off the southern head, at the river's mouth, is a castle-like rock which, at high tide, is partially surrounded by water. It is the ancient fortress of Te Kawa, which withstood many an assault.

The hills south of Tongaporutu begin to drive in a massive wedge

between the road and the sea, great towering slopes and cliffs leaning over the road as if the King Country is making a last, forbidding gesture; at the hamlet of Ahititi (which means "Fire for Cooking Mutton Birds") the road is forced to climb steeply to escape the enfolding arms of Mount Messenger, a complex of sandstone pinnacles and ridges fleshed in puggy soil and clothed in dark forest, where the southern frontier of the King Country lies at 189m (620ft) above sea level amid a splendour of bush-covered ridges and magnificent scenery, on the northern edge of Taranaki.

Taranaki might well be described as the country of the immigrant mountain and immigrant men. According to legend, there were once three great mountains in the centre of the North Island. They were Tongariro, Ruapehu and Taranaki. Taranaki began flirting with the beautiful, forest-clad wife of Tongariro, the peak Pihanga, and Tongariro and Taranaki quarrelled and threw fireballs at one another, until Taranaki fled westward, until he came to the tip of West Cape.

Now Taranaki is called Mount Egmont, and his real name has been given to the province in which he stands, and which he seems to have drawn up around him like a blanket. Egmont's graceful cone is visible from every part of Taranaki which, from its outermost corners, rises up towards the lovely peak. Inevitably, Egmont has been called New Zealand's Fujiyama, though it s not quite so perfectly symmetrical as Fuji. Nevertheless, the mountain is a splendid sight, whether seen framed in a tracery of bush from New Flymouth's exquisite Pukekura Park, or rearing above the lush farmlands around Inglewood and Stratford. Driving south from Mokau and Tongaporutu on a clear day, you may see Egmont dead ahead, looming over the capes and headlands of the north Taranaki coast, an angle from which he appears as a perfect cone, for his great out-thrust shoulder, Fantham's Peak is on his southern side.

South of Mount Messenger, the land gentles, with hedged pastures of vivid green slipping down towards the cliffs, coves and black ironsand beaches of the coast, rolling inland towards the higher, wilder inland hills, and always lifting, hill, dale and river valley, towards Mount Egmont. Near the small village of Urenui there is a low, bush-covered ridge, out of the side of which pokes what appears to be a canoe prow bursting forth from a green wave. This is the now overgrown site of Okoki *pa*, an ancient fortress, and the "canoe prow" is a memorial to Sir Peter Buck (Te Rangihiroa), a chieftain, perhaps the greatest authority on Polynesian history and culture in the world and a fine scholar and historian who, by precept and example, did much towards putting new heart into the demoralised, diminishing Maori race at the turn of the century. With a body of other spirited and determined young men, he formed the Young Maori Party, and worked to give his people a new political awareness and to revive in them a vital interest in their ancient culture. Now his ashes rest, with those of his wife, in a stone-walled hollow behind the monument.

From Urenui to Waitara, the road dips and zooms over low, rolling hills and valleys that go down to the coast. It runs through Waitara, where stood the *pa* of Wiremu Kingi te Rangitaake, Paramount Chief of the Ngati-Awa tribe, who went to war with the Government in 1860 in an effort to prevent his land from being sold by two dissident chiefs, Teira and Kirikumara. From there it runs along a section, known as the Devon Line, to New Plymouth, today a city in which many of the old landmarks that Wiremu Kingi and the settlers knew have been swept away. The Huatoki stream still flows through the centre of the town as it did in 1860, when it assured the besieged citizens of a water supply, but today it runs deep underneath streets and buildings; and even the Devon Street bridge, where the public notice board used to relay the orders of the military to the civilians under their protection has disappeared. In 1860, the main part of the town lay behind defensive entrenchments spread about the foot of Marsland Hill, on which stood the military barracks. The trenches encompassed Fulford, Vivian, Powderham, Courtenay, Devon, King and Gill Streets, from just west of Queen Street to Liardet Street. Now, only the old maps show where the defensive works ran, though at the foot of Marsland Hill the original St Mary's Church, the garrison church, still stands, enlarged since those days, and surrounded by graves which tell of violent death. The church is decorated inside with the hatchments of famous regiments and corps, its wooden pillars, carved from whole *puriri* trees, bearing brass plaques recording the gratitude of some early citizens for sanctuary during those troubled and unsettled times.

Looming over the church, Marsland Hill is now a pleasant park, small but commanding a magnificent view of this little city which curves around a rugged coast and reaches back into valleys shaded by fingers of forest. Here stands a monument to those who fought in the New Zealand Wars, carrying the names of all units.

In the streets adjacent to St Mary's are many old houses and buildings dating from New Plymouth's beginnings. And at the entrance to Brooklands Park is The Gables, designed in the Tudor style by that Frederick Thatcher who designed Howick's All Saints Church in Auckland. The Gables, built in 1848 to the order of Governor Sir George Grey, was a hospital, originally serving Maoris for the most part, but used as a military hospital during the wars. It was removed from its original site some years ago, re-erected at Brooklands Park and restored as a hospital. It gives an accurate and amazing picture of the remarkably high standard attained by a frontier-town hospital built six years before the Crimean War, when

Above, top: The sea is steadily eroding away the coast at Tongaporutu, north of New Plymouth; in one great cavern out by the sea are early Maori rock drawings
Above: The memorial, in the shape of a war canoe prow, to Sir Peter Buck (Te Rangihiroa) at his birthplace, Urenui

The fields of dairy farms come right to the cliff edge on the coast north-east of New Plymouth, where the beaches at the cliffs' base are of black ironsand

Florence Nightingale gave birth to the modern concept of hospital standards. (It is interesting to reflect that its first resident surgeon bridged the gap between the military medicine of the Waterloo period and the beginnings of modern practice, and that he was actively opposed, on good, scientific grounds, to the use of anaesthetics.)

Another Thatcher design, the Old Vicarage in Courtenay Street East, is a stone building, erected in 1845. Cut into the stone are the arms of the Church of England in New Zealand, a simple design of three stars on a shield. This is the earliest example of Church of England arms existing in New Zealand, and is known with carefree irreverence as "The Bishop's Brand".

Brooklands Park contains the wondrous Bowl of Brooklands, an open-air theatre where tiered seats look across a still lakelet to a sound-shell stage backed by native bush. The Bowl of Brooklands has remarkably good acoustics, the pool is like a mirror, and to ballet, operatic, orchestral or choral performances is lent an out-of-this-world, dreamlike loveliness which is a most moving experience. New Plymouth holds the Festival of the Pines each summer, providing a programme by both international and national artists, with plays, variety shows, musicals and symphonic orchestral recitals in the Bowl of Brooklands.

Near to the centre of the town is Pukekura (Red Ochre Hill) Park, a unique garden and sports ground. The sports ground is set in a natural amphitheatre, and the gardens are superb. Here is the remarkable Fernery, where terraced glasshouses are interconnected rather ingeniously by tunnels; and the Rhododendron Dell, which is a riot of changing colour from early August to late November.

From the Kiosk overlooking the lake is obtained a famous view of Mount Egmont, awesomely beautiful as it stands framed in native bush.

Carrington Road, which slips almost secretly out of the southern suburbs of New Plymouth, creeps past ragged fields and twists and backtracks its way through increasingly dense bush, before straightening out and coming to Pukeiti "The Little Hill".

"In Pukeiti," says the booklet issued by the Pukeiti Rhododendron Trust, "a few men found a habitat for their imaginative dreams. The vision was of rhododendrons scattered amongst but not engulfing a sanctuary of native trees, plants and birds. . . ." And that, in essence, is the story of a handful of men of a generation which had grown weary of eroded hillsides, the rotting stumps of old burnings and the unchecked spreading of gorse, blackberry and pig-fern on the lower slopes of Mount Egmont which was the legacy of the first enthusiastic but unskilled attempts to tame the land hereabouts. They decided to rebuild a forest, a natural garden of primeval splendour, tamed only to the extent that it would be threaded through with well-kept paths and occasional beds of small plants. Into this glorious setting it was planned to introduce rhododendrons of all kinds. Now, the Pukeiti property, administered by the Trust, is like a great artist's palette of colour, with the delicate shadings of azalea and camellia, the brilliant splashes of rhododendrons and the general background of native evergreens.

The park is divided into blocks, each with its special layout and particular attraction. There is the Azalea Block, the Camellia Block which includes scarlet oaks, Japanese maples, prunus, lilacs and gingko trees, the *Kauri* Block where ninety young *kauris* are thriving, the Hybrid Block with its nursery of many species of rhododendron, and the Pukeiti Hill Block, where splashes of rhododendron contrast colourfully with the native bush, and from which a fine panoramic view can be obtained of New Plymouth, the green and brown farmlands and the shining expanse of the Tasman Sea.

Pukeiti was here before Mount Egmont came on the scene. It did once have an earlier tall neighbour, a volcano named Pouakai, which blew itself to pieces in successive eruptions until it became a jagged, truncated cone, scarcely recognisable as a cone at all. The bones of the hill Pukeiti were covered by Pouakai's ash, and by ash from the slowly building Mount Egmont. Streams running off Pouakai deposited silt, plant life invaded the area, and decaying vegetable matter added life-giving elements to the volcanic soil. Pukeiti and its vicinity was, in former times, a great source of red ochre, or *kokowai*, used by the Maoris as a colouring agent. Since European occupation, samples of this red ochre have been made into paint, but presumably – and fortunately – it was not considered profitable enough to exploit.

Pukeiti forest contains some fine examples of many native trees, notably the strange *rata* tree, which begins life as a parasitic growth in the crotches of large forest trees. When this site no longer provides sufficient nourishment, aerial roots are sent down to the ground, and these eventually coalesce into a massive trunk. In many cases the dead host can still be seen, forming the rotting core of a huge *rata* tree.

The beautiful cone of Mount Egmont rises above the native bush and the lake of New Plymouth's Pukekura Park

Mount Egmont

Mount Egmont has, high on its flanks, a number of lodges, notably the Dawson Falls Tourist Lodge, a delightfully Swiss-styled hotel. The road up to Dawson Falls turns in through a concrete gateway which marks the boundary of Egmont National Park, and climbs steadily up the mountainside through some of the most beautiful forest on earth. This is the haunt of *karearea*, the New Zealand falcon, commonly referred to as the bush hawk, the *piwakawaka* (fantail), and other small birds, notably the tiny *titipounamu*, the rifleman, 6cm (2½in) long and appearing to have no tail. He is to be seen climbing up and down the branches and trunks of trees, clinging effortlessly to the rough bark, picking out insects. *Tui* and *korimako* (bellbirds) abound, as well as *kereru*, the native pigeon, and *miromiro*, the tomtit.

At one point in the easy climb, through the gap in the trees can be seen Dawson Falls, named after one Thomas Dawson, who discovered the

126

The Lodge at the Pukeiti Rhododendron Trust, 360ha (900 acres) of park and bird sanctuary

lovely cascade while tracing the source of the Kapuni river in 1883. The Falls may be viewed, of course, from closer vantage points and better angles. In fact, the entire mountain may be explored on walks of up to 17 hours' duration. The walk to the summit is particularly rewarding, for from there the lower slopes appear as a dark-green, blanket-draped circle of slopes falling away to the dappled, valley-riven lowlands. To the west, the Tasman Sea is a dark, flecked blue stretching away to the distant horizon. To the east, Mounts Ruapehu and Ngauruhoe stand, snowclad peaks shining in the sun, sometimes appearing to rise like the mountains of some Jack-and-the-Beanstalk land across a nubbled, rolling cloudscape.

The forest on the higher slopes includes mountain fivefinger, the undersides of whose leaves are silvery by contrast with the darker topside foliage, a fact which gives rise to a peculiar and beautiful phenomenon. When wind blows over the face of the mountain, its passing can be traced by a pale flash which moves across the mountainside as fivefinger leaves turn over. From a distance, it is as though momentary and wavering

Dazzling white in its blanket of winter snow, Mount Egmont rises over the rich farmland of Taranaki

Bush, trees and ferns combine to create this typical lush piece of Taranaki rain forest

streaks of colour chalk-mark this high-level forest.

The mountain tussock of this region is another natural wonder, looking from a distance to be orange-red, yet proving when examined close up to be a definite green.

The last eruption of Mount Egmont can be dated very accurately by an examination of *kaikawaka* trees just above a ski lodge, Stratford Mountain House, on the eastern slopes. The trees have short boles and wide-spreading branches. The soil contains a layer of pumice which, when it settled on the slopes, killed most of the vegetation. A comparatively few sturdy *kaikawakas* survived. The effect of the pumice was to check their growth – hence the short boles – and their wide spacing encouraged a great spread of branch. By taking a core of wood out of the living tree and examining its growth rings back to the first ring indicating a reduction in growth rate, it has been possible to date the last eruption back to 1555. However, Egmont is not an extinct volcano, but a dormant one, and may erupt again some day.

The view from Dawson Falls Tourist Lodge is enchanting. Sometimes, when it is raining on the mountain, it is sunny and fine on the plain below, a sight which is glimpsed through a miraculous golden veil created by the rays of early sun playing on the edge of Egmont's weather. But perhaps the most entrancing view is caught at night, when the constellations of the little towns are coruscating in the darkness far below – Stratford, Eltham, Hawera, Patea and, faint and far, a mere line of hazy light on the south-eastern horizon, Wanganui.

The South Taranaki Coast

The skirts of Mount Egmont come right down to the sea on its western side. Villages nestle in sheltered valleys, including Omata, Oakura and Tataraimaka, the latter famous as the locality in which the Hauhau faith had its genesis, invented and propagated by a half-demented Maori seer, one Te Ua Horopapera Haumene, who began having strange dreams and portentous visions. (Horopapera, incidentally, is the Maori form of Zorubabbel.) He put together a series of strange rites and chants which, he claimed, were given to him by Anehera Kaperiere, the Archangel Gabriel, but which owed much to the Church of England Book of Common Prayer, the Book of Revelation and his own bemused imagination. The old *tohungas*, all but ousted by the Christian faith, embraced this strange new religion as a means of welding the tribes together and fanning the flames of nationalism to a heat fierce enough to revive the flagging war spirit of a discouraged people. It embraced ritual cannibalism, the taking of heads and all manner of fearsome practices, and it was called *Paimarire*, which means, oddly enough, "Good and Peaceful", a faith which, stripped of its savage practices, exists in modified form to this day.

Tataraimaka, today, has chosen to forget the tragic fanaticism which sprang from its vicinity, and the gully which once hid ambuscade and sudden, screaming death now contains a store and a dairy factory; the inhabitants call it Tatra-mack, and regard it simply as a very ordinary place of work and residence.

At Okato the country begins to flatten out towards the coast, albeit with a sprinkling of curious, small, conical hills, formed by debris which was deposited around huge blocks of lava during a vast mud-flow when Egmont was active.

The slightly undulating plain widens around the southern skirts of Egmont and becomes more intensely cultivated farmland dotted with small settlements. From the first of these, Opunake, Egmont is now seen to have two peaks, the second one being the shoulder and pinnacle of Fantham's Peak. Opunake is a popular beach resort, its small, symmetrical curve of sand enclosed in a semi-circle of tall cliffs. The plain inclines slightly upward to the base of Egmont, and on it, notably near Kapuni, oil wells produce hydrocarbons, in the form of natural gas. Natural gas is also taken from undersea wells out from the coast. It is used for the production of nitrogenous fertilisers, and for lighting and heating in industry and homes, being piped to New Plymouth, Auckland and Wellington.

There are many mementoes in this part of the country of the tragic wars of the 1860s. Manaia, about 32 kilometres (20 miles) south-east of Opunake, preserves a redoubt with watchtower and blockhouses; and north-east of Manaia, in a special reserve, is a reminder of earlier, tribal wars, the great Turuturu-mokai *pa*, of which only the massive earthworks remain. The *pa* was conquered by the Ngati-Tupaea Tribe about three hundred years ago, and its palisades and defensive ditches could still prove a formidable obstacle to modern infantry and tanks.

Spreading over the lovely valley of the Wanganui river, Wanganui city has developed enormously from the piece of riverside land the New Zealand Company bought from the Maoris in 1840

Wanganui and the
Wellington West Coast

The War Memorial Tower on Wanganui's Durie Hill offers splendid views over the city and the surrounding countryside as far as Mounts Egmont and Ruapehu

Wanganui is situated at the mouth of the great Wanganui river. The business heart of the city lies between two sandy hills, now public parks, known as Queen's Park and Cook's Gardens. In the days of the Hauhau troubles, when a Hauhau attack down the river threatened, these hills were occupied by twin fortresses known as Rutland Stockade (Queen's Park) and York Stockade (Cook's Gardens), and at times as many as 800 soldiers were garrisoned in the area.

Queen's Park, once known to the Maoris as Pukenamu ("Sandfly Hill"), forms as attractive a centrepiece as can be boasted by any city, a place of sloping lawns, balustraded steps and shady trees, with splendid public buildings, including the Alexander Library and Museum, and the Sarjent Art Gallery. The museum contains many fine Maori artifacts, including a superb collection of weapons, and two great *waka-taua*, or war canoes: *Te Wehi-o-te-Rangi* ("Anger of the Skies"), nearly 19m (61ft) long, carved out of a single *totara* tree at Taringa-mutu about 140 years ago, and *Te Mata-o-Hoturoa* ("The Face of Hoturoa", Hoturoa having been captain of the *Tainui* and ancestor of many of the river people), about 23m (75ft) long, with a beam of nearly 2m (5ft 6in). About 120 years old, she was used in the wars of the 1860s, and bullet holes can still be seen in her hull.

Cook's Gardens, a mere two city blocks away, is a natural amphitheatre – or one aided only slightly by man's artifice. It has become for New Zealand athletes almost a national shrine, for it was here that the New Zealand runner, P.G. Snell, set up a new world record for the mile on 27 January 1962.

Durie Hill, which overlooks the river and the city, is distinguished by a stone tower, the War Memorial Tower, a rather medieval-looking

Pretty Jerusalem (Hiruharama) saw the beginnings of Mother Mary Joseph
Aubert's Order of the Daughters of Our Lady of Compassion

structure with a crenellated top and arrow-slit windows. It is reached by
an elevator, a remarkable and unique lift to which access is through a
220m tunnel. It rises from street level to the top of the hill, a height of
65m (216ft), in about 60 seconds. The tower is 31m (103ft) high, and
commands a sweeping, panoramic view of the city, the river, the farmlands and forested hills to the far skirts of Mount Egmont, the coast of
the South Taranaki Bight, which sweeps in an immense curve southward
towards Kapiti Island, and the rumpled, densely bush-covered country
which climbs towards Mount Ruapehu in the far-off centre of the island.

135

The Wanganui River

The Wanganui river used to be described as the Rhine of New Zealand. Steamboats used to ply the river, from Wanganui up to Taumarunui, which, though almost at the centre of the North Island, was a thriving port. It used to be the principal route in to Taupo and Rotorua.

To see the river today, it is necessary to take a road which winds along its bank, though this turns inland at Pipiriki, before the truly grand scenery is reached.

The river flows down to the sea past a series of Maori settlements originally established as mission stations by the Rev. Richard Taylor, who was fond of bestowing Biblical names on them. The first such station upstream from the mouth he called Athens, which the Maoris rendered as Atene. The next, predictably, he called Corinth, which still exists, no longer a mission station, of course, but a settlement of pleasant little cottages set amongst the fruit trees, around the neat little church. The Maoris call it Koroniti. Farther upstream still, and departing from the Biblical precedent, is London. It will never reach the proportions of its great namesake, which is as well, because it is a pretty place; the Maori

Above: Kapiti Island, a bird sanctuary, rises dark, steep and densely forested
6.4 kilometres (4 miles) off the Manawatu coast
Opposite: A beautiful stretch of the Wanganui river, here flowing between bush-
clad hills, with the central mountains of the North Island beyond

version of its name, by which it is commonly known, is Ranana. The fact
that it was given a non-Biblical name was not due to any change of heart
by Richard Taylor, but to the fact that it was not one of his missions, but
a Catholic village. There is still a mission school in Ranana, perched up
on a hillside above the village, operated by the Congregation of the
Daughters of Our Lady of Compassion.

Upstream yet again from Ranana is Moutoa Island, on which the last
great battle of the Wanganui river was fought between loyal Maoris and a
force of Hauhaus trying to go through their territory to attack Wanganui.
On 14 May 1864, the opposing forces met on Moutoa Island, and while
Brother Euloge, a Catholic missionary, knelt and prayed for Divine aid,
they set to. Brother Euloge was killed where he knelt. There is a
memorial to the dead in Wanganui.

A little over 6 kilometres (4 miles) from Ranana is Jerusalem – or, to
give it the lilting Maori form of the name, Hiruharama. This is not
Jerusalem the Golden, but Jerusalem the White and Green, set against a
hillside overlooking a broad bend on the river, where willows crowd down
to the placid water and a rocky bluff across the river stands like a
sentinel, crowned with tall poplars, and with *kowhai* trees that drip golden

The Manawatu coast sweeps in a broad curve of sandy beach past the small town of Paekakariki

flowers. Jerusalem, too, is a Catholic village, its mission station founded in 1883 by Father Soulas, a priest from Hawke's Bay. In that same year there came to assist him Marie Henriette Suzanna Aubert, a brilliant Frenchwoman who had studied medicine at a time when a woman had to sit behind a screen when attending lectures; and she had served as a nurse on a troopship during the Crimean War. In 1899 she founded the order known as the Congregation of the Daughters of Our Lady of Compassion. Mother Mary Aubert – Meri, the Maoris called her – worked long and hard at Hiruharama, and in many other parts of the country, notably at Wellington, where the Daughters opened a home for the incurably sick and maimed. She brought more and more sisters from the Wanganui river to help in the Wellington work, and the blue habit with the white peasant coif with its goffered frill around the face became a common and well-loved sight in the capital. She died in Wellington at the age of ninety-two, and her funeral cortège was one of the longest ever seen in that city. Rich and poor, halt and lame, priests, nuns, ministers and people of other churches, judges and prelates followed her to the graveyard. Government offices closed, and sittings in the Supreme Court itself were postponed on that day. And, of course, the Maoris came in their hundreds, to deliver the most touching farewell of all.

"Go, Meri! Go, Lady! Go to our Father and to our Ancestors. Go to those who held the faith in the days when you lived among us and ministered to our bodies and to our souls. Go! Mother of the orphan and the poor. Go to our Lord. . . ."

Today the Order maintains nine Homes of Compassion in New Zealand, Australia and Fiji. And it all began here, at tiny Hiruharama, Jerusalem, on the Wanganui river.

Pipiriki, the next settlement, is almost dead. For some years there was a fine accommodation house here, catering for passengers on the steamship service.

The river, from Wanganui up to Pipiriki, flows between hills alternately forest-clad and clothed in pasture. From Pipiriki northward it presents scenery of spectacular beauty, with no fewer than ninety rapids and many narrow gorges. At Pipiriki, the first hint of what the upper reaches are like is given, with forest-crowned, rocky pinnacles, and bluffs which are furred with fern.

The Wellington West Coast

South of Wanganui, the land rolls back from the coast, tree-patched and fertile, excellent farmland, flattening gradually as it spreads down to the Rangitikei river. The coast sweeps in a clean, gently shelving curve around the South Taranaki Bight with, here and there, vast stretches of sandhills, which undulate like ocean waves in almost every direction over a kind of desert which stretches from just south of the Wangaehu river to the Rangitikei river.

The fine, sandy beaches reach southward in an unbroken curve, except for where the Rangitikei, Manawatu and Ohau rivers spread out across the sands, down to the magnificent west coast resort beaches of Paraparaumu, Waikanae and Raumati, sheltered from the full force of the Tasman Sea gales by the lofty, forested bulk of Kapiti Island.

The traveller going south from Wanganui sees little of this tract, however. The main route is by Bulls, through Sanson and Foxton, or with a slight deviation via Palmerston North. Palmerston North (there is another Palmerston in the South Island) is the principal town in the Manawatu/Rangitikei area. Flat, with some pleasant, tree-lined streets, this small city is probably most attractive at its centre, where the shopping and commercial area is laid out around a large, gardened square. Like Rome, it is the North Island city that all roads lead to, with routes passing through it between Auckland and Wellington, Taranaki and Hawke's Bay, which lies on the eastern side of the Ruahine ranges.

The Manawatu river actually flows out to the west coast through a deep gorge, a narrow gap between the southern end of the Ruahines and the northern end of the Tararuas. On the whole, it is a gentle river, which has worn its way down as the ranges have risen up, maintaining its westward flow over aeons of time. It is understandably boisterous as it carves its way through the gorge, but it forgets its mountain turbulence as it rolls peacefully across those last kilometres of flat countryside to the sea.

Near Levin, the mountains begin to swing towards the coast until near Otaki, they seem almost to lean over the town. At Otaki ("The Place of the Staff Stuck in the Ground"), the old chieftain, Te Rauparaha, evidently deciding that, like Alexander, he had no more worlds to conquer, turned at last to the Christian religion. He had seen truly marvellous church buildings in Australia, and determined to build a church at Otaki. He called it Rangiatea, the Maori form of Raiatea, that idyllic isle near Tahiti from which the *Tainui* had brought his ancestors. Indeed, beneath the church is buried a portion of the sacred earth

Wellington's rapidly expanding commercial centre dominates this view of New Zealand's capital, built on the steep hills around Port Nicholson

brought by those ancient immigrants from Raiatea over six hundred years ago. The church still stands, well used.

Te Rauparaha died at the age of 81, and was buried in the church grounds; but in the night his body was exhumed and taken over to his old stronghold, Kapiti Island, probably because he had wished it, and on his deathbed entrusted the task to old friends. Few, if any, Maoris and no *Pakeha* know exactly where his body lies buried. His monument, however, stands in the churchyard.

Kapiti Island is a bird sanctuary, which is one reason why tourists are not actively encouraged to visit the place. It is understandable, because not only are its birds curious, friendly and often quite unafraid, but also, Kapiti, rising out the Tasman Sea like a Gibraltar, is forested and precipitous, dangerous for people unaccustomed to steep bush where an unwary step can mean a fall over a high precipice.

From time to time, grim remains of Te Rauparaha's grisly feasts are discovered on Kapiti: charred human bones, broken open so that the marrow could be extracted.

Modern buildings rise in cliff-like masses over Lambton Quay, one of
Wellington's main business and governmental streets

At Paekakariki ("Perching Place of the Green Parakeet") the hills
come down close to the sea, paddling their feet amongst the rocks and
reefs which here begin to supplant the swept, clean sands of the beaches.
So close do the ranges come to the sea that the road and railway scramble
over their toes, dipping and climbing and swooping along narrow, carved-
out ledges on rocky, bush-clad faces. Road and rail are never, therefore,
very far apart, and run together into Pukerua Bay and Plimmerton, seaside
settlements crouching in the mouths of valleys which run back from rock-
bound bays and inlets, often taking the sea with them; and road and rail
climb over or tunnel through a ridge and come down to Porirua Harbour,
shallow, tidal and landlocked, and Porirua city sprawling about it and
climbing over its sheltering hills, all the way to Titahi Bay.

There is a long inlet running eastward from Porirua Harbour into the
deliciously peaceful little hamlet of Pauatahanui, where Te Rauparaha's
cousin and principal co-belligerant, Te Rangihaeata, "The Dawn of Day",
once had a mighty *pa* on the sloping site where now stands the little
church. Artists, poets and other writers favour this area, and many office

workers and professional people from Wellington commute into the capital from here every day.

The eastern suburbs of Porirua are pleasantly sited around Titahi Bay, a crescent of golden sand protected by rocky headlands, facing out to Mana Island, smaller and lower than Kapiti, and covered with grass pastures for sheep.

From Titahi Bay southward, the coast is a narrow strip of interrupted reef and short stretches of beach, backed by tall, steep hills, mostly grazed by sheep. The coast curves fairly sharply south-eastward at Cape Terawhiti, where a lighthouse marks the entrance to Cook Strait, and the long, steep, parallel ridges march across a high peninsula, and come down to the shores of Wellington harbour.

Wellington

Wellington is the capital city. Its physical development has been governed to a very great extent by the nature of the land. The flat areas of the city, at Te Aro and Thorndon, could accommodate only a severely limited number of people, since it also had to serve as the business and shopping area and, once it became the nation's capital, find room for an ever-growing army of civil servants as well. Building on the surrounding steep hillsides was difficult and costly and is so today, which undoubtedly accounts for the fact that the hillsides facing inwards to the harbour are covered by large areas of rather quaint Victorian and Edwardian villas, still occupied as dwellings. Many have been altered, modernised, added to and generally transformed, not once but many times, until they resemble no one architectural style, but are apt to incorporate Victorian sash windows, obscure-glass doors *circa* 1940, ornately plastered ceilings, modern wrought-iron balustrading and the very latest wall-bracket electric lights mounted on fittings which used to carry gas lamps. It is simply that it has proved economically impossible to tear them down, and successive generations have made shift with them. It probably could not have happened in any other city but Wellington; but nobody really lives in the capital. That is to say, about nine out of ten people, when asked, prove to be living in Wellington only because they have been transferred to their head office from some branch, that they are really from Hawke's Bay, or Manawatu, or Taranaki, or the Waikato, to which they have every intention of returning. Perhaps, in the final analysis, few do return, because Wellington is a delightful city in which to live.

Those picturesque old villas are a part of its charm. Many are still unspoiled, and there is undoubtedly something about the houses of middling-prosperous businessmen of the late Victorian or Edwardian period. They tend to have tall windows flanking a balcony or a glassed-in porch upstairs, and a polished brass doorstep, big, ornate door knocker and stained glass upper panels in the front doors. They awake a happy nostalgia. Everybody's grandmother lived in a house like that.

But the flat land around the waterfront was soon crowded with the buildings of government and commerce. Land was reclaimed between Te Aro on the southern side of the harbour, and Thorndon on the western side, which served the two-fold purpose of allowing more building along the waterfront, and of taking the quays out to deep water, so that ships could berth alongside, instead of having to discharge on to lighters out in the roadstead. Lambton Quay, which had followed the old shoreline, became a much sought-after site for business houses, hotels and shops.

Today, the main business thoroughfares are Lambton Quay, which

142

The best views of Wellington and its surroundings are from Mount Victoria; this one is looking north-west across Oriental Bay and Lambton Harbour

Old St Paul's Cathedral in Wellington, was built in the 1860s to a design in
Early English Gothic style by the Rev. Frederick Thatcher

runs in two gentle curves from the Cenotaph at Bowen Street near that
peculiar addition to the House of Parliament known sardonically as the
Beehive, through an area occupied by banks and insurance houses, to join
the long, straight stretch of Lower Willis Street; Willis Street itself, lined
with large department stores, small boutiques and arcades, begins to climb
slightly where Manners Street darts off to the left, narrow, bustling and
crowded with shops; Cuba Street, which runs at right angles across
Manners Street, and seems to be to Willis and Manners Streets what
Karangahape Road is to Queen Street in Auckland; and Courtenay Place,
wider and flatter, and ending at Kent Terrace, where Queen Victoria's
Jubilee Statue stands, and which suddenly sneaks off around the harbourside to Oriental Bay.

Between the harbour end of Cuba Street and the Railway Station at
Thorndon is a tangle of queer little streets, not so much laid out as
having happened in haste, where second-hand bookshops and auction
marts are being gradually squeezed out by high-rise office blocks.

Actually, the crowded business area, where Victorian and Edwardian
buildings with corniced and columned formality are being replaced by
equally pretentious truncated skyscrapers of concrete and glass, is becoming too crowded for comfort, creating draughty canyons; and the new
buildings themselves often – and more and more – have to scramble for a
precarious footing along steep terraces at the foot of the harbourside hills.
Yet they all, old and new, manage to combine to give Wellington a
specially endearing quality. Viewed as a whole, the centre of the city is

Battalions of tulips, which have their own "Tulip Day" every October, herald the arrival of spring in Wellington's Botanical Gardens

an engaging mixture of tall commercial buildings and bright store windows, consequential and somewhat self-conscious governmental buildings, Gothic Revival churches standing in the shadows in little, twisty streets, and colourful noisy main thoroughfares interconnected by dimmer lanes where old houses are still occupied, and suburban-style grocery stores and the shops of Chinese traders and importers may be found.

Viewed from some height such as Mount Victoria, or from the air on a clear night, Wellington possesses an almost magical beauty. The hills are a filigree of light about dark and tree-filled valleys. The long Hutt Valley at the harbour's head is a river of light, which divides to encircle the glistening black water of the harbour like a jewelled diadem.

The western suburbs of Wellington spread out over the steep ranges of still partially forested hills, some of them once isolated villages connected to the inner city by a steep road which wound – and still winds – its way through deep, narrow valleys and up precipitous slopes. Now Tinakori Road has acquired vast networks of equally steep tributary streets, and from the suburb of Kelburn a cable car descends through tunnels and past quiet streets hung on a hillside, to the hurly-burly of crowded shopping streets.

Modern development has meant that many of Wellington's historic and really interesting buildings have been destroyed; but on the same hill as Parliament House, tucked away in a little network of streets of old houses, is the old Cathedral of St Paul the Apostle. There is, closer to the seat of Government, the new Cathedral of St Paul, rather stark and modern, though with a grace and beauty of its own; but the old cathedral,

Between the sands and reefs of Wellington Harbour's Eastern Bays, and the forested faces of the Orongorongo Range, is the delightful suburb of Eastbourne

standing in Mulgrave Street, is a beloved shrine, bound inextricably into the Dominion's history. Old and wooden, it is aged enough to have seen that instrument of rough justice, the stocks, in use. It is built on land jointly donated by Bishop Selwyn and Sir George Grey in 1861. On the site already stood an old wooden church, whose Vicar, that architect-priest the Rev. Frederick Thatcher, declared it so dilapidated as to be irreparable. He designed the original portions of the Cathedral Church, but its construction evidently left something to be desired. The boisterous Wellington winds caused the building to pitch and rock, accompanied by a positive screaming of tortured iron bolts and straining timbers, to such an extent that on one occasion it almost drowned out the choir. Transepts were added, extra bracing was arranged, more rafters and spandrills were added – and, miraculously, with all this tampering and bolstering by architect and engineer, the building emerged as a harmonious whole, and one of the finest examples of New Zealand Colonial Gothic architecture still in existence. It possesses some very fine stained glass, a fine altar of *kauri* and *puriri* and a Bishop's Chair which has carved on it, curiously, a Latin inscription which reads "Arthur John, Abbot of Glastonbury".

Across the broad Thorndon end of Lambton Quay from Parliament House is the old Government Building, claimed to be the biggest wooden building in the southern hemisphere, and one of the biggest in the world. The original specification called for "permanent materials", but in this earthquake-prone land, timber semed to be more trustworthy – so it was built of wood, with one-and-a-half-inch thick weatherboards milled and shaped to look like blocks of stone.

On the crest of the ridge overlooking Te Aro stands the Dominion Museum and Art Gallery and before it stands the Carillon, the National War Memorial, from which its 49 bells ring out on Anzac Day and on days of national rejoicing. It towers above the city, its eternal lamp burning as a faint star at its top. (It was not put out during the days of blackout in World War II, but its glass was painted over.) Beneath it is the Hall of Memories.

Finest of all Wellington's parks, where Wellingtonians love to stroll or to drowse on green lawns while a band plays in the sound shell, the Botanical Gardens are a network of winding paths which meander down ferny valleys and over pine-covered spurs, and scramble up steep hillsides through native bush. The paths take sudden twists into places with deliciously scarey names like Druid's Hill, where the wind sighs and whispers through the pine trees even on a still day; or they climb gentle steps through the delightful Camellia Garden, or debouch on to the green Magpie Lawn, seemingly remote from the ceaseless traffic which flows along Glenmore Street beyond the wrought iron fence.

Two of the Gardens' chief delights are the Norwood Begonia House – of which one American visitor remarked: "It's the loveliest thing I've seen. Not just the loveliest begonia house, but the loveliest *thing*!" – and the Lady Norwood Rose Garden, a circular garden, strictly formed, with a fountain and a perimeter of pergolas. In its siting, with that graceful, well-mannered, gentle formality backed by a steep hillside rough and dark green with pines and lush native bush, it typifies colonial New Zealand as few other places do. The Rose Garden and the Begonia House, genteel and, somehow, rather Victorian, finding themselves cheek-by-jowl with a wild and alien beauty of tree ferns and native evergreens, decide that they will settle down with unaltered, well-bred habits, and simply co-exist. And, as it did with the Colonists, it comes off!

It was of Wellington harbour that the comment was made that it could hold the world's navies in perfect security. Today that would most assuredly be an exaggeration; yet it is still an immense and wonderfully sheltered haven. It was – and correctly still is – called Port Nicholson, which the old whalers shortened to "Port Nick", and the local Maoris, liking the sound of the name, Maoriied into "Poneke".

The bay around which the city curves, and in which the docks have been constructed, is called Lambton Harbour, the eastern side of which curves around Oriental Bay to Point Jerningham. Oriental Bay, marshalled into a tidily embankmented parade, fenced and planted with spaced Norfolk pines, is overlooked by tall apartment buildings between which are squeezed narrow old villas. Tucked into its curve is a sandy beach, laboriously built there with sand carted from better-endowed shores, for the enjoyment of the citizens. Around Point Jerningham, the long arm of Evans Bay reaches down to an isthmus which was once the entrance to the harbour, until a great earthquake, ages ago, threw it up and opened a new entrance to the east of the Miramar heights. Point Halswell marks the eastern extremity of Evans Bay, and from its lofty tip the coastline runs down past a series of shallow indentations – Scorching Bay, Karaka Bay and Worser Bay – to Palmer Head and the reef-bound western side of the harbour entrance.

The harbour has two islands, Somes Island, which is a quarantine station, and Ward Island, largest of a cluster of rocks standing out from the harbourside settlement of Eastbourne.

From Palmer Head, the outer coastline runs in a northward-tending curve, the beach and suburb of Lyall Bay, separated by a long finger of land from the double curve of Island Bay, sheltered from the storms of Cook Strait by Taputeranga Island, and from whose confetti-scatter of cottages and larger houses can be seen, hazy on the southern horizon, the snowy peaks of the South Island.

The Marlborough Sounds, at the north-east tip of the South Island, are a
paradise of sheltered inlets, many accessible only by boat

Marlborough and the Kaikoura Coast

Above: Kenepuru Sound, the eastern-most of the network of inlets which make up Pelorus Sound, has several fine holiday centres
Opposite: The harbour at Picton, the busy Marlborough Sounds town which is the South Island terminus of the Inter-Island ferry service

Picton and the Marlborough Sounds

The hills which rise across Cook Strait from Cape Terawhiti are part of a labyrinth of land and waterways known as Marlborough Sounds. The tall ridges are a continuation of the mountainous wedge between the Wairau river valley and the Waimea valley, a tangle of ridges and spurs and peaks, several of them 1524m (5000ft) high, known as the Richmond Range. At its northern end the range was drowned, partly due to the rise in sea level after the ice ages, but also to a vast subsidence, evidenced by the fact that the entire block is still tilting down into Cook Strait.

According to Maori legend, certain gods came down from the heavens in a canoe, straying too far from their sources of power to be able to return. The canoe capsized, which is not altogether surprising even for a superhuman canoe, in the wild waters of the region, and the carving of its shattered prow forms the Sounds.

No one can be certain, but it is most likely that Captain Cook was the first European to sail into the Sounds, coming down from the stormy Tasman Sea, his ship foul with many months' growth of marine ex-crescences. It must have been with considerable relief that he discovered what he described as a "snug cove", which he named after Queen Charlotte, George III of England's consort, and in a broad, forest-fringed bay which became known as Ship Cove, he careened and cleaned his ship.

He also claimed the entire mainland for Great Britain, hoisting the Union Jack at the top of Motuara Island. He climbed the larger, higher Arapawa Island, and saw "the eastern sea", the Pacific, which, he was

150

pleased to note, was connected to the Tasman by the broad waterway which he called Cook Strait.

Queen Charlotte Sound is one of two principal waterways which comprise Marlborough Sounds. The other is Pelorus Sound, explored in 1838 by another British Naval Officer, Lieutenant Phillip Chetwode who, perhaps a little less dutiful than Cook, named the Chetwode Islands near the mouth of the sound after himself, and the sound itself after his ship, and be blowed to the Lords of the Admiralty.

The largest of the many branching sounds is Kenepuru Sound, perhaps the most beautiful of them all, 15 kilometres (9½ miles) of landlocked, wonderfully sheltered waterway, with a wealth of small, bush-surrounded coves, where the days are musical with the chime of *tui* and bellbird.

The port of Picton nestles into the mouth of the deep valley which runs inland from the head of Queen Charlotte Sound. This is the southern terminal of the Cook Strait Rail Ferry service, which doesn't enter the sound at its northern end between Cape Jackson and Cape Koamaru as Captain Cook did, but through the narrow Tory Channel on the eastern side of Arapawa Island.

Picton is very small, but was nearly bigger. Sir Edward Stafford, one of New Zealand's most able Premiers, was almost successful, in the nine-

From the summit of Botanical Hill there are splendid views of the countryside surrounding Nelson

teenth century, in persuading parliament to make Picton the capital. (Many South Islanders will say that they wish devoutly that he had succeeded.) In the end, though, it didn't even succeed in becoming the capital of Marlborough province. Parvenu Blenheim, better sited, in the centre of fertile, easy farmland, was preferred.

It does, however, have the distinction of being named after one of the Duke of Wellington's commanders at Waterloo, Sir Thomas Picton, the hero of Badajoz, who was killed while blocking the otherwise open road to Brussels with his Scottish infantry.

Where the hills stop and the Wairau Plain begins, so does some of New Zealand's finest wine country. The Wairau valley is sheltered by high ranges, the annual tally of sunshine hours is almost ideal for wine grapes, and the soil is splendidly fertile, and watered by the Wairau's numerous tributary creeks. Between the Main South Highway and Kaituna to the west, the landscape is the Old Testament ideal, where every man may sit "under his own vine and under his fig tree, and none shall make him afraid". Which is a happy issue out of such early afflictions as the horrific massacre perpetrated on a group of surveyors and intending settlers by Te Rauparaha and Te Rangihaeata on 17 June 1843. (There is a monument to them near the main road, at Tuamarina, a name which is a corruption of a Maori word which can be translated as "Calm Past", surely one of the least appropriate names in the country.)

The Kaituna valley is a pleasantly bucolic area of picturesque farmsteads, orchards and sheep in a valley so sheltered, so kindly gathered in by the ranges, that its gentle climate seems to have been at pains to preserve the old cob cottages of the pioneers. No longer inhabited, they nevertheless still stand here and there beneath sheltering old trees. But behind the scene of peace and quiet husbandry are the rugged ridges and forested spurs which climb up into the Richmond Range. This is the limit of the hospitable, open land, and from here the way plunges into wild

CHURCH HILL

1842

A sunny place for lunch on the steps of Nelson Cathedral

scrub and denser bush. Now and again the hills relent and stand back watchfully about quiet, grassy valleys and small hamlets: Havelock, peaceful and, not untidy, precisely, but of a comfortable country casualness, relaxing at the head of Pelorus Sound; Canvastown, where a few houses and an hospitable pub are all that is left of a once rip-roaring mining town; Pelorus Bridge in the Rai valley, spanning a delightful dell in bushland which may still be the habitat of the *kokako*, variously known as the Orange Wattled Crow, the Organ-bird (from his long note of song), and the Gill-bird. The species is not rare, exactly. The northern, blue wattled *kokako*, is quite widely distributed, but this orange wattled sub-species is now scarce, the last acknowledged sighting being in 1962, though there have been unconfirmed reports of its presence since then.

The main highway climbs over the Whangamoa Saddle, 357m (1170ft) high, through a gigantic tumble of forested hills, coming down to the eastern shore of Tasman Bay and running into Nelson city.

Nelson is the South Island's northernmost city. It isn't very big, having a population of somewhere around 30,000 in its urban area. It has been a city, however, since 1858, even though it was not big enough at that time even to qualify for borough status, and continued to be not big enough for another sixteen years after that. But Queen Victoria said it

Above: The centre of New Zealand – as indicated by this memorial on Botanical Hill, Nelson
Opposite: Arrow Rock, in Nelson Haven, is sometimes called "Fifeshire" after the immigrant ship wrecked here in 1842

was a city, and made it so by Letters Patent, bless her heart, and no one could argue with that. Furthermore, she ordained that it should be a Bishop's See, and so it was, and is.

Physically, Nelson is an attractive place. Sheltered from the cold blast of the southerly winds by high hills, it curls itself about their feet, leaning towards the sun and dipping its toes into the warm waters of the bay. One learns from the map with some slight surprise that it is very little south of Wellington, and that it seems well justified in its claim to be the geographical centre of New Zealand.

The town's focal point is its cathedral – to give it its full style, Christ Church Cathedral, Nelson. It stands on Church Hill, on the site of a fortification erected at the time of the Wairau Massacre, rather like a close column of troops, with its tower standing out in front like an officer. It is an interesting building, being vaguely Romanesque from the transepts forward, except for the pointed arches, included evidently to give some degree of uniformity with the nave, which is most decidedly Gothic Revival. The doors are rather fine, promising the grandeur of a soaring Gothic nave, a promise which is not fulfilled. The walls of the nave rise in Gothic dignity, pierced by narrow stained glass windows, but carry no clerestory or vaulted arches. Instead, a low-pitched roof spans the nave, and the chancel and the sanctuary are plain to the point of starkness,

154

modern-looking and, indeed, austere by comparison with the nave. It looks rather as if it had been designed by a committee. The reason for this abrupt and, let it be said, surprisingly harmonious marriage of styles was the great Murchison earthquake of 1929, which called into question the whole business of building codes in the area. Amongst other restrictions, the new regulations precluded the building of clerestory and vaulted nave. The cathedral stood incomplete and temporarily roofed for many years until at last a determined Chapter got it finished and consecrated.

From the cathedral steps, Trafalgar Street runs straight down to the sea, one of Nelson's main business and shopping thoroughfares, from whose seaward end is obtained a superb prospect of Church Hill, the graceful steps and the four-square cathedral tower.

Nelson, at its centre, contains many delightful, unspoiled colonial houses, genteel little old ladies of houses, as Victorian as can be, a feature which it shares with New Plymouth, though Nelson's houses are more original in appearance, and there are more of them. (There is, incidentally, an historic connection between the two cities. At the time of New Plymouth's siege in 1860, many families were brought as refugees to Nelson, and settled here.)

All the gardens seem to have lemon trees, and all the streets seem to be named after Admiral Lord Nelson's victories and after his associates.

Rock strata exposed by wind and sea add drama to the coast line at Ngaroa Bay, west of Nelson

The way to the Centre of New Zealand lies across the shaven grass of a playing field, beginning between two enormous Monte Carlo palms and winding up a steepish path, a twenty- to thirty-minute climb to the crest of Botanical Hill, where a concrete block bears the legend "N.Z. Survey 1877" and its cast metal frame is inscribed with the official pronouncement that this is, indeed, the centre of New Zealand.

The summit, in spring, is glorious with jonquils and daffodils. At one's feet lies a tangle of shrubs and dense growth of native and exotic trees. The view is superb, and confirms that Nelson is a very small city. To the west lie Queen's Gardens, and to the left, about ten o'clock, Nelson College, an historic boys' school, spreads its mellow buildings across a green terrace. A straggle of houses drifts past the school, through the valley where the road runs to Stoke. The valley itself is bounded on the east by the Grampians, lying sprawled and rumpled, humped like a sleeping beast. You can walk over them if you enjoy a steepish track, the smell of gorse and the occasional dramatic grouping of stands of dark pines. The path meanders delightfully on to Flaxmoor, nearly 396m (1300ft) above sea level.

To the east, the road runs alongside the Maitai stream, through its deep and tortuous valleys, to the Maitai Reserve, from which a track runs over Maungatapu ("Sacred Mountain") to Havelock. This was the original road to Havelock, debouching, eventually, into the Wairau valley. It was on Maungatapu that the notorious robbers, Burgess, Levy and Kelly murdered travellers nastily for their gold, or whatever money they might be carrying. They were sentenced to death and their death masks are now in the Nelson Museum, taken after they were hanged, disturbingly puffy sets of features with bulging eyes. Sullivan, the fourth murderer, turned Queen's Evidence and was pardoned. Later he was found guilty of yet

Isel Park at Stoke, Nelson, contains fine trees planted over a century ago by wealthy landowner Thomas Marsden

another murder, and sentenced to penal servitude for life.

The museum also contains a pewter plate from the men's messroom on HMS *Victory*, inscribed around the rim with the words:

"Britannia Triumphant Her Navy Invincible, Her Intrepid Nelson Victor at Aboukir, Copenhagen and Trafalgar Where He Gloriously Died in the Moment of Victory, Oct 21st, 1805".

Here, too, are relics of the Wairau Massacre, and a simple wooden cot, significant only because it was once occupied by a child who was to change the whole world – Lord Rutherford, father of nuclear science, who was a Nelson man.

The Maitai stream broadens to a river as it approaches the sea. Boats lie at anchor in it. A long spit known as Boulder Bank reaches a protective arm about Nelson Haven, into which the Maitai flows. Beyond the bank, calm and blue, Tasman Bay spreads across to Separation Point, behind which lies Golden Bay.

Within the shelter of Boulder Bank, the Maitai, the Brook and other, smaller streams have deposited silt which has built up into a tidal mudflat, across which, at low tide, the smaller streams wander in serpentine loops and the Maitai runs deep; from a little distance to the east of its mouth, down to the old entrance to Nelson Haven, near Arrow Rock, between Haulashore Island and the mainland, there are marked channels for shipping. On Boulder Bank is a tiny white lighthouse of classic design, made of cast iron, prefabricated in England and erected on Boulder Bank in 1861. The entrance to the harbour is now through a dredged channel between Boulder Bank and Haulashore Island.

The main road north from Nelson actually starts out in a southerly direction, running around Magazine Point and past Tahunanui Beach and its tidal lagoon, to the village of Stoke, now more or less a suburb of

Broadgreen, built in Nelson in the 1850s in the style of an English Victorian farmhouse, carefully preserves the furnishings of that by-gone period

Nelson. Stoke is a place of apple cider and apple wine. (The difference between cider and apple wine is held to be the alcoholic content, cider being under 15% proof and wine over 15%.)

Two old homesteads in this area which repay inspection are Isel Park and Broadgreen. Isel Park Homestead is now a museum with a certain doll's-house charm and a magnificent garden, and Broadgreen, which is a pure delight, is a cob house, the earth for its construction having been dug out of what now forms its cellar. It is dainty with dormer windows, and a children's room where, one imagines, little Victorian children once sat curled up with a story book in the window alcove in the thick wall. The dining room is splendid, the whole house homely and comfortable, able to be lived in exactly as it is, without alteration or addition, though it was built in 1855.

Around the curve of the bay, where the road at last turns northward over slightly undulating land, orchards spread around Richmond and Appleby on the fertile Waimea Plain, at the northern end of which the country rises up to form long ridges parallel to the shore. Between them runs the Moutere valley, good wine country; and beyond the valley, where it opens out into a large area of flatland where apples and pears are grown, orchards and farmlands spread out around Motueka, the principal township. A few kilometres to the north of Motueka is the village of Riwaka, strung out along the road, surrounded by hop orchards whose conical oast houses line the route.

A side road climbs in a wide curve around a range of scrubby hills to Kaiteriteri, a beach resort of great beauty; but the main way climbs up over Takaka Hill, a mountain of more or less solid marble, whose skeleton thrusts out of the rough, bracken-tufted earth near its 828-metre (2715-foot) summit. There is a marble quarry about three quarters of the

158

way up, and near it is the "new" Ngarua Cave, recently furnished with proper walkways and electric lighting, well worth a visit for the almost unbelievable delicacy of its formations. Almost at the summit is the turnoff to a plateau known as Canaan, a weird area of twisted marble outcrops like demonic sculpture, typical karst topography, with sink-holes and ancient caves which, with the gradual tilting of the land, have become vertical shafts of frightening depth. The deepest chasm in the southern hemisphere is here, known as Harwood's Hole, a fearsome pit of darkness whose main entrance is guarded by cliffs 100m (300ft) high. There is a stream somewhere down there in the blackness, which comes out into the Takaka valley on the northern side of the hill. The caves are

The golden sands of Kaiteriteri Beach help make it one of the loveliest and most popular beaches in Nelson

inhabited by a species of beetle, a Tolkienesque creature which, living all its life in total darkness, has no eyes.

From the top of Takaka Hill, the road makes a 10-kilometre (6½-mile) winding descent to Upper Takaka and the Takaka valley, a narrow strip of rolling, gentle country, a green patchwork quilt of fields and shelter-belts of trees, with the Tasman Mountains looming above them like a dark wall.

The Takaka valley runs down to Golden Bay through these pleasant farmlands, where diminishing patches of *totara* and *kahikatea* (white pine) serve as shelter breaks. The valley widens near Takaka township, in the vicinity of which is a locality called Anatoki ("Cave of the Axe"), where tame eels, enormous, muscular-looking creatures thrust their black, shiny bullet heads out of the water to receive from a resident benefactor a sumptuous repast of meat, sago and blancmange. New Zealand eels are reputed to be the world's biggest, and these are monsters even by New Zealand standards.

Also in the vicinity are Waikaremumu Springs, popularly known as Pupu Springs, possibly the world's largest known freshwater spring, with a reputed 2,200 million litres (475 million gallons) of water welling up

Above: In the Anatoki river south of Takaka the tame eels will take food from visitors' hands
Opposite: Memorable for its bleak roughness, gaunt dead trees and outcrops of weathered marble, the Caanan Road branches off Takaka Hill

every twenty-four hours. The source of the spring is not known, though there is a measurable increase in volume when it rains heavily in the Takaka area; but research has revealed that the water, when it first bubbles up clear and icy cold, has not been exposed to air for a period of from three to five years.

North-east of Takaka, the coastline is spectacular, with great lime-stone bluffs crowned with native bush entwined with wild passionfruit. At Ligar Bay is the Abel Tasman Memorial, a shining white obelisk and tablet on a railed platform overlooking a beautiful bay with a long sweep of sand, from which green farmland tilts back to the forested ranges, where the ridges and spurs of Abel Tasman National Park come down to Totaranui and the southward trending chain of inlets and coves marking the park's coast. Separation Point, just beyond the park's northern extremity, marks the southern end of Golden Bay, once known as Murderers' Bay because it was here that some of Tasman's crewmen were killed when attacked in their longboat by Maoris.

The northernmost town in the South Island is Collingwood, a small town sitting on the shore of Ruataniwha Inlet, beyond which the coastline sweeps up in a long curve to Abel Head and Farewell Spit, a 36-kilometre (22-mile) sand bar which curves out towards Cook Strait from the northernmost point of the Island. Cape Farewell is a place of cliffs, and of fierce winds which romp in off the Tasman Sea. A hundred million years old, according to geologists, the quartz sandstone which forms the mighty bluff has been carved into a cyclopean archway, and the crumbled spoil of the ocean's carving curves away from the foot of the cliff to form the spit. The Cape is pitted with caverns of pink rock; bird-

161

The memorial to Abel Tasman, who reached New Zealand shores in December 1642, gazes out over Golden Bay from a clifftop east of Takaka

The blood-red bottlebrush flowers near the Tasman Memorial seem to recall
Tasman's crewmen killed by Maoris in Murderers Bay

crowded islets dot the coast, and a colony of seals lives a life of slothful
ease in a secluded and hard-to-reach bay.

Farewell Spit starts at Fossil Point. It is about 1 kilometre (½ mile)
wide, a strange place of wandering dunes up to 30m (100ft) high, from
the top of which the wind whips a spray of sand like the spume from the
top of an ocean wave. There are quicksands and *raupo* swamps, and 6½
kilometres (4 miles) of mud flats on the southern shore which are covered
with fatal swiftness by incoming tides. Bird life on the spit includes bar-
tailed godwits (*Limosa lapponica*), called *kuaka* by the Maoris. They find a
sanctuary there between September and March, when they migrate to
their breeding grounds in Siberia, half a world away and an unthinkable
distance for so small a bird. Hundreds, possibly thousands, of black swans
also gather there for safety during their flightless season.

Cape Farewell and the Spit were seen and charted by Abel Tasman in
1642, but it was not until 1770 that Captain Cook named them, taking

The beach at Totaranui, the information and accommodation centre for the Abel Tasman National Park, established in 1942 on the north-west corner of Tasman Bay

Blenheim, often called the "Sunshine Capital" of New Zealand, is built on the Wairau plain on the banks of the navigable Opawa river

one last look, as he was leaving New Zealand.

The clump of macrocarpas and pines on the low part of the Spit was planted in the 1870s by a lighthouse keeper named Harwood who was concerned that although the lighthouse warned most ships away, some of the more low-lying stretches were invisible from the sea. So every time he brought out supplies, he brought two saddlebags of earth, and was eventually able to plant the trees, which are now considered to be at least as valuable as the light itself.

Blenheim and the Kaikoura Coast

Thirty kilometres (18½ miles) south of Picton, Blenheim is a rapidly-growing market and food-processing town, to whose industries has recently been added that of winemaking.

Blenheim is a comfortable town, still rather old-fashioned, though charmingly so, with an ornate band rotunda in the middle of its surprisingly spacious Market Square, from which the streets radiate in all directions, a most unusual layout for a New Zealand town, and one which suggests that the town grew haphazardly around its once all-important wharf, for Blenheim was, until quite recent times, a river port.

From Blenheim, the main road southward travels out across the

The mountains come down to the sea on the coast between Kaikoura and the delta of the Clarence river, with the Seaward Kaikouras rising beyond the coast hills

Wairau Plain, clambering through the complex of fairly high hills which wall the plain on the southern side, and coming down again to the terraced flats about the Awatere river. The way skirts Lake Grassmere, a tidal lagoon on the sea coast and site of a solar-evaporation-type saltworks which produces sufficient salt and salt products to meet most of New Zealand's needs. Grassmere is an eye-catching jewel of a lake, especially when seen from the air on a sunny day, with its turquoise blue and dazzling whites set in the midst of a rolling, brown countryside.

The road is a switchback sort of highway, running between the curve of the Haldon Hills and the abrupt wall of Limestone Ridge, and coming down to the coast at the Ure Bridge, so called because the river it spans was once named after the Ure river in Yorkshire; but, as often happens in New Zealand, the original Maori name, Waima, prevailed. It means "White Water", a reference to the river's limestone bed.

For some distance south from Ure Bridge, the coast is windswept, with salt-browned fields running between the gravel beaches and the steep hills, forming a narrow shelf dotted with bent shrubs and wind-tormented trees, and cabbage trees whose fronds are ragged and burnt sere and brown at the tips. Isolated farms and an attractive little stone church are well spaced out from one another along this rather desolate coast.

But presently, where the hills degenerate into crumbling cliffs and stand somewhat closer to the road, the Clarence river issues from its long, curving, narrow valley between the Seaward and Inland Kaikoura ranges, lofty chains of peaks, snow-crowned for much of the year and awesomely, over-bearingly close. The river, freed from those confining walls, spreads out over a boulder-strewn flat, forcing the road to turn inland to find a narrow reach of the river which can be more conveniently bridged.

South of the Clarence and its little settlement, in the region of Black Miller Creek, the land begins a series of counter-attacks against the battering Pacific, a series of outward thrusts which culminate in the Kaikoura Peninsula. Forbidding cliffs frown over the ribbon of coast road, the wind-burnt scrub clings desperately to rocky faces, and the railway, sharing the same narrow shelf with the road, dives through a succession of tunnels and concrete shelters designed to shield it from falling rocks.

Just past Iron Gate, a cruel promontory of jagged, cavern-riddled rock, a scenic drive of considerable merit runs up to Blue Duck Valley, where the Blue Duck stream chatters companionably through a native bush reserve in which many species of native bird can be seen, and glades of sylvan beauty delight the eye, all sheltered from the ocean wind and out of earshot of the constant roar of the sea on that turbulent coast, behind the densely forested ridges.

The main road also presently leaves the coast for a while, and slides across a hedged and meadowed plain, bypassing the town of Kaikoura. Kaikoura itself consists of a street of quaint shops, small hotels and pretty houses, with a breathtaking backdrop formed by the Seaward Kaikoura Range, peaks of which soar to over 2744m (9000ft) in places, yet trail their skirts in the sea. From Kaikoura their height makes them appear closer than they really are, for a fairly flat and very fertile plain lies between the town and the mountains, with a slightly rumpled bit of downland between the southern end of the town and the Kowhai river.

The Kaikoura Peninsula thrusts out from the mainland rather like a clenched fist with pointing index and little fingers. It is a place of grassy downs perpetually ruffled by the wind, deep gullies, tall cliffs and a rim of

Strong winds from the vast Pacific Ocean twist the trees to strange shapes
and whip up the sea into immense waves all along the exposed Kaikoura
coast

Hanging stalactites reach down to meet stalagmites growing from the floor of the
Maori Leap limestone caves south of Kaikoura

sandy, reef-sheltered bays. Here came the invading Ngai-Tahu people
(whose name can be translated as "The Beloved People") to dispossess the
Ngati-Mamoe; and here came Te Rauparaha, on vengeance bent, to take
utu – repayment or revenge – for the insult of a Ngai-Tahu chief. The
name of the place, Kaikoura, means "Feast of Crayfish", which have
always been plentiful here.

Captain Cook, who lay becalmed off the peninsula, found his ship
Endeavour attracted canoe-loads of Maoris who, when anyone tried to
engage them in conversation, just gaped and remained silent. He called
the place "Lookers-on". But the Maori name has stuck to it, not least
because the chief in these parts when white settlement of Canterbury
Province began, was also named Kaikoura, and was a giant of a man in
every way.

Not that Kaikoura is in Canterbury province. It is in Marlborough,
the southern boundary of which is to the south, down a road which
returns to the sea coast south of the peninsula, near the Maori Leap
Caves, whose stalactite formations are like dripping toffee in shades of
honey and amber, and the fossilised bones of seals and penguins suggest
that the cave was once much closer to the sea. The route skirts another
strip of rockbound coast, running through a tunnel to negotiate one rocky
bluff, and presently climbs into high hills, swooping down at one point to
a bridge which is high above the Conway river, Marlborough's southern
boundary.

The formal grid pattern of Christchurch's streets with the green mass of Hagley
Park in the centre

Canterbury

Although the Conway river forms the southern boundary of Marlborough, it does not form the northern boundary of Canterbury, as many people imagine. In fact, Canterbury's northern border is 45 kilometres (28 miles) to the south. The intervening tract of land, hilly, well wooded in places, watered by some twenty sizeable streams, innumerable creeks and one major river, the Waiau, is properly part of Nelson Province. Most of the long, comparatively narrow strip which runs out to the east coast was once a single gigantic sheep run belonging to a man named Robinson, known as Ready-Money Robinson, who earned the nickname by paying for his land in hard cash. He called his estate Cheviot, and on the coast he built a small port, which he called Port Robinson. Eventually the land was cut up into smaller holdings for closer settlement, and a town was built, at first named McKenzie after Sir John McKenzie, Minister of Lands, who had acquired the land for breaking up, and who built the town. But the settlers eventually took to calling the town Cheviot, which suggests a sneaking admiration for Robinson, a man whom the history books suggest was a bit of a curmudgeon.

Tamed since Robinson's day, the land is fairly flat around the town, which is in a basin surrounded by high hills. The Lower Peaks Range, which rises to heights of 878m (2850ft), separates this basin from another higher and larger basin of equal quality and equally intensive cultivation, which cradles three townships, Waikari, Culverden and Hawarden, and through which runs the highway to Lewis Pass, northern route to the West Coast, and Hanmer Springs, a delightful spa resort in the midst of glorious mountain scenery.

This appendage to Nelson province is bounded south of Cheviot by the Hurunui river which, in fact, is Canterbury's northern boundary. From the Hurunui southward, the country is rolling, sometimes steepish pastoral land, which eventually flattens out to the Canterbury Plain.

The plain begins as a comparatively narrow coastal strip at Waipara, twisting away inland from the coast just north of Amberley, a small hamlet whose beach resort marks the beginning of Pegasus Bay, a smooth, sandy curve of beach sweeping southward for nearly 65 kilometres (40-odd miles), interrupted only where the Ashley and Waimakariri rivers spill out into the bay, and terminating in a last, long sandspit on the estuary of the Avon and Heathcote rivers at the base of Banks Peninsula.

The coastward villages of Leithfield, Waikuku and Woodend have holiday settlements of the same name on the coast, connected to them by long roads which are more like country lanes. A network of roads runs inland from them to Rangiora, a sizeable country town, and Oxford, once a timber-milling town and a health resort, but now the centre for a farming community. Kaiapoi lies nearer to the coast, and was once hopeful of being Canterbury's principal port, for its river is navigable for small coastal vessels. But shipping ceased to call when Canterbury's major and original port of Lyttelton was connected to the principal city, Christchurch, by a railway tunnel.

Christchurch and Banks Peninsula

Christchurch, sprawling about the foot of Banks Peninsula and scrambling up its steep sides, is New Zealand's second-largest city, with a population in excess of a quarter of a million. It was founded by an organisation called the Canterbury Association, which itself was begun under the auspices of Edward Gibbon Wakefield's New Zealand Company. It was to be a Church of England settlement, and the site originally chosen was

Hill country farming in South Canterbury: sheep graze in the paddocks of a farm near Fairlie

Above: Christchurch's Bridge of Remembrance was erected in 1923 over the
Avon river, named after a river in Ayrshire, Scotland
Opposite: Spring comes in with a wealth of blossom and daffodils in
Christchurch's central sport and recreation area, Hagley Park

Port Cooper, a fine, deep harbour at the base of Banks Peninsula which
opened out into Pegasus Bay. The association received a great deal of help
and encouragement from Lord Lyttelton, who was its chairman in
London, and when he suggested that they might call the new colony's
capital Lyttelton, they agreed readily. But Lyttelton proved unsuitable for
expansion, too restricted topographically for real growth, and the site of
the capital was moved over the hills and on to the plain. Since the
harbour had already been called Lyttelton, the new town was called
Christchurch, after the Oxford college of the association's real leader and
man-on-the-spot, John Robert Godley.

The centre of Christchurch is Cathedral Square, but the Avon river,
which loops and winds through the inner city, is its heart. More than
that, the Avon is Christchurch and Christchurch is the Avon. For the
Avon meanders along at an easy-going pace – and so does Christchurch.
The Avon dreams for long stretches through tree-shaded, graceful suburbs
and green parks, sauntering in slightly impudent imitation of bigger
streams with older names, and carries it off rather well, as does Christchurch. The Avon divides around sudden islands, curls in improbable
loops, brawls in an unmannerly way through a bottleneck or over a weir,
surges swiftly and slows as readily to a crawl, like Christchurch traffic and
Christchurch life. It seems, somehow, to express that quality of life which
is uniquely Christchurch's, which bigger Auckland and noisier, brasher
Wellington cannot match.

The Avon's bridges hint at the city's particular qualities – quaint little
bridges, wide enough for modern traffic even though some were built a
century or more ago. They look clean and demure, often wearing lacy
white iron railings, all curlicues and spiky finials and, with their ribbons
of deep blue handrail, look like little old ladies from another age.

There are exceptions. Cashel Street bridge is not of their genteel
company, though it is equally beautiful. It is the Bridge of Remembrance,
a war memorial, set here because over the original little bridge men
marched away from the adjacent King Edward Barracks to fight in various
wars. The Bridge of Remembrance is spanned by a tall, graceful arch. It is
no longer used by motor traffic, but is tiled, with steps going down to
Cambridge Terrace, a bridge to walk over, taking one's time.

The planning of the high-minded Anglican founders of the city
envisaged an English-style public school for the sons of the gentry, the
clergy and such other boys as might, by diligence and merit, attain to a
classical education. It was to stand hard by the university, the chapel of
which would be the city's cathedral; and the entire complex was to form
the centre of the city. In the event, it was held that the city centre was
much too valuable a property for anything but commerce, and with a fine
disregard for the plans and dreams of the founders, the City Council and
the Provincial Government ordained that the Church should establish its
educational foundation and its cathedral somewhere else. In the case of
the public school and the university, the Church complied, with the
happy result that the public school, Christ's College, stands, all grey
Gothic dignity, on the banks of the Avon, its dormitories and its masters'
quarters looking out at North Hagley Park, and the university buildings
occupy a block on the other side of the road, a delightful collection of
structures with interesting roof lines, doorways and turrets, and flights of
steps which carry the eye along its facades and lead it into intriguing
alleys and passageways, affording glimpses into monastic-looking cloisters:
a flourish of Gothic liveliness which positively invites you to explore.
And explore you may, for Canterbury University has long since outgrown
these quarters, and moved out to a somewhat soulless, vast complex in

the western suburbs, and the old university is now an arts centre, with theatres, craft shops, and the like. At its western end, it faces across Rolleston Avenue where the statues of the City Fathers stand, to the Botanical Gardens.

The Gardens cover an area of some 30ha (62 acres) of quiet, tree-shaded walks which seldom stray far from the Avon, itself alive at weekends with canoeists.

The Canterbury Museum stands beside the Rolleston Avenue entrance to the Botanical Gardens, with the McDougall Art Gallery backing on to it. The Museum is justly famous for its ornithological exhibits and for its splendid Antarctic section. It also contains a full-scale representation of a Christchurch street of the mid-nineteenth century, through which one may go window shopping, even entering into some of the shops; and a goldmining town, complete with bar and bank and, greatest triumph of the display artists, a smithy wherein the blacksmith is hammering away at a horseshoe which glows red hot, while beads of sweat stand out on his brow, and the muscles cord on grimy hands and powerful forearms.

The one building that the civic authorities failed to banish from the city centre was the cathedral. They persuaded a determined bishop to move the site from the western to the eastern side of Cathedral Square, but that was as far as he was prepared to go. The foundation stone was laid in 1864, the first service was held in a tent within the unfinished walls, and the completed building was consecrated in 1881. It was designed by Sir George Gilbert Scott, an English architect said to be the greatest exponent of Gothic Revival and the greatest ecclesiastical archi-

Above: The wooden church of St Michael and All Angels, completed in 1872, replaced the hut built by the first Anglican settlers in 1850
Opposite: Christchurch Cathedral's copper-sheathed spire rises over Cathedral Square, proclaiming its place at the centre of an essentially Anglican settlement

tect of his time, though the on-the-spot architect who supervised the construction was one B. W. Mountfort, who was to Christchurch what Sir Christopher Wren was to London. Of particular interest in Christchurch Cathedral is the High Altar and reredos, a carven glory in richly golden *kauri*, which was salvaged, with a fine eye for fine timber and appropriate symbolism, from the old Hurunui road bridge, at the northern boundary of the province and the diocese. The view from the balconies on the tower take in the city, the plains and, on a clear day, the Southern Alps, from a height of 37m (120ft) above the tile-paved, traffic-free concourse of Cathedral Square. The spire stands 66m (215ft) high.

The design of the cathedral was said to have been inspired by Caen Cathedral in Normandy, and the French influence is apparent in the semi-circular apse.

Not far away the Church of St Michael and All Angels, often referred to as the Mother Church of the Plains, was the first church built in Christchurch, and actually served as pro-Cathedral, where the First Bishop of Christchurch was enthroned. Built of wood, it contains some fine interior woodwork, and has numbered pews, the rear five rows being marked "Free", a relic of the days of pew rentals.

Of the other, now numerous, churches in this Church of England colony, two are particularly outstanding. One is the Parish Church of St John, in Latimer Square, another fine Mountfort edifice, the foundation stone of which was laid in 1864. It was, as a matter of fact, the first stone church to be built on the Canterbury Plains – by the Masonic Order, which mistrusted the Anglo-Catholicism of St Michael's.

The other notable church is not an Anglican church at all, but the Roman Catholic cathedral in Barbadoes Street, a very fine building in the Roman Renaissance style, designed by Frank Petrie, a home-grown architect of considerable note. The Cathedral of the Blessed Sacrament, standing back from the street in generous grounds in Barbadoes Street, was described by George Bernard Shaw in the 1930s as "the finest church south of the line". (He upset some of the touchier Anglicans by adding, with typical Shavian offensiveness, that he did not mean the church in the square, but the one "down by the gasworks".)

But it is the collection of Mountfort buildings that constitute Christchurch's most favoured architectural heritage. He built the Provincial Council Chamber, a delightful little wooden and stone Westminster, whose passages are floored with worn stone flags and headed with low, dark beams, and whose Council Chamber is still in its original condition, with fatly-padded, stoutly-buttoned leather upholstery, splendid Speaker's Chair and spacious press and public galleries to proclaim its importance and bespeak its massive and ceremonial dignity as the parliamentary

Above: Christchurch's stylish Town Hall complex, designed by local architects
Opposite: The splendidly Victorian Gothic interior of the Provincial Council
Chamber in Christchurch, built in 1865

wranglings of its members seldom did. It has a magnificent barrel-vaulted
ceiling, painted and gilded with Gothic designs by a Frenchman named St
Quentin, who used to be hoisted aloft at the beginning of each day with
his paints and a bottle of cognac, and let down again at day's end.

Newest of the city's public buildings – as distinct from commercial
edifices – is the Town Hall, which rises on the banks of the Avon,
looking from across Victoria Square like a modern artist's impression of
Windsor Castle.

Christchurch began in the vicinity of Cathedral Square, and was
designed to be four-square, bounded by four avenues and traversed by
streets running strictly east–west and north–south. But the same cussed-
ness which ousted higher learning and ecclesiastical consequence from the
square also foiled the planners. It is all very well to have a neat, four-
square plan; but when citizens wish to travel from home to work-place, or
down to the river for water, they are apt to ignore the official streets and
go across the empty subdivisions by the shortest route; and shrewd traders
naturally build shops along the lines of daily migration, to catch their

From the Port Hills, the first settlers beheld an 11-kilometre (7-mile) width of swamp laced with small, reed-choked streams

trade. So although most of the streets of inner Christchurch conform to the neat pattern, there are thoroughfares like High Street, or Oxford and Cambridge Terraces, that meander unabashed across the plan on winding or diagonal track, which can be confusing in an absolutely flat city.

Not quite absolutely flat. Banks Peninsula rises up abruptly on the edge of the plain. That part of its steep hills which climbs away from the city is known as the Port Hills, because they separate Christchurch from its port; and the suburbs which spread over the face of the hills begin at Westmoreland, and run around through Cashmere, and Heathcote to Mount Pleasant, Redcliffs and Sumner.

Sumner also occupies the flat shelf between the Port Hills and the coast, and is really rather older than Christchurch. A great mass of lava, slowly sinking into the Sumner sands, is known as Cave Rock, obviously because it is pierced through with caverns, and carries on its summit a small stone signal station and mast, no longer used but once charged with the task of signalling to small trading vessels the state of the Sumner Bar, where the estuary of the Avon and Heathcote rivers runs out into Pegasus Bay. A short distance upstream, a port was established at Heathcote, and from it the first railway built in New Zealand ran into Christchurch. There is a museum of transport and technology there now, for the port died when the railway tunnel was dug through the rocky core of the Port Hills to Lyttelton.

Banks Peninsula was named by Captain Cook after the botanist, Sir Joseph Banks. He did not call it Banks Peninsula, however, but Banks

Pleasurecraft moored in one of the many bays and anchorages around Lyttelton Harbour

Island. With the estuary on its northern side, and an 11-kilometre (7-mile) breadth of swamp around its base, it looked like an island to Cook. And it was an island, long ago. It was the fierce rivers carrying gravel down from the crumbling young mountains that built up the Canterbury Plain, which ultimately reached out into the comparatively shallow continental shelf and captured the volcanic island. Geologists say it happened aeons ago, though there is a locality on the inland side which was called Tai Tapu by the Maories. Tai Tapu means "Sacred Shore".

At all events, two major volcanic peaks reared up, connected by a criss-crossed webbing of ridges and minor peaks. Both exploded with titanic force, and the sea eventually entered the craters, which now form Lyttelton Harbour and Akaroa Harbour. The origins of Lyttelton Harbour, which first comes into view as you drive over the pass by the Sign of the Kiwi roadhouse, are immediately apparent. The ancient crater is still ringed by the eroded but still impressive rim, with its jagged contours and its formations of twisted lava.

Nestled beneath its western rim is Lyttelton, an old town, a colonial town, a multi-coloured spatter of houses reaching up the craggy crater wall. As well as the rail tunnel, there is also a road tunnel from Lyttelton through to Christchurch.

Akaroa, on the southern side of the peninsula, is some 80 kilometres (50 miles) by road from Christchurch, a road which runs across the very edge of the plain, sometimes climbing across the spurs of the Banks Peninsula hills, insinuating itself between them and the broad expanse of

The former French settlement of Akaroa nestling beside its quiet harbour on Banks Peninsula

Lake Ellesmere, a shallow tidal lagoon about 160 square kilometres (60 square miles) in area. The road turns in from the area between the lake's edge and the sea coast, runs in through a narrow valley between Lake Forsyth and the high hills, passes through the village of Little River, and climbs up over the eastern rim of the crater which forms Akaroa Harbour.

Akaroa was originally a French settlement; today, its streets have names such as Rue Balguerie and Rue Viard, and many of its old houses have lacy wrought-iron balconies and a generally Gallic flavour.

At the head of the harbour is the locality known by the lovely name of Duvauchelles, and there are other localities around the peninsula shores with names like Le Bons Bay and French Bay and French Farm. But today's inhabitants, even those who are direct descendants of the original settlers, are English-speaking New Zealanders, and Duvauchelles has become "D'voshels", and all that really remains of French Akaroa is a faint, lingering memory, like a hint of perfume hanging on the air. (Other racial beginnings and languages have likewise succumbed. The point named by Danish sailors Snefellness, meaning "a promontory surrounded by a snowfield", has become Snufflenose.)

The gorge of the Rakaia river, one of the great rivers which have built up the Canterbury plains

Timaru and the MacKenzie Basin

From the alpine foothills which ring the Canterbury Plain for a hundred miles four great rivers come down: the Waimakariri, the Rakaia, the Ashburton and the Rangitata. There are others, such as the Selwyn, but the Selwyn, along its middle reaches, flows underground, seeping seawards through its bed of gravel, not surfacing until it reaches the seaward plain, across the last few kilometres of which it flows, deep and placid, into Lake Ellesmere. The major rivers are broad, gorse-patched braids of tangled waterways, often swift, deep and dangerous.

The hills gentle as they swing out towards the coast at the southern extremity of the plain, becoming round and green and fat, with hedgerows, English trees, and pretty villages tucked into their folds, as restful as a day in bed. The South Canterbury coast is, for much of its length, a long stretch of gravel beaches backed by tall cliffs of yellow conglomerate, from which the billiard-table-flat pastures run back, looking like a landscape which has been cut along its edge with a knife.

South of the Rangitata, the downs begin to lift higher in an almost

Sheep graze on the grasslands around Springfield, a small farming community on the road up to Arthur's Pass

semi-circular complex of more or less gentle folds, enclosing a slight bulge in the coastline – it hardly seems definite enough to be called a promontory – in the northern, sunward curve of which lies Timaru.

Timaru is a resort town, its seaside streets overlooking the beautiful short curve of Caroline Bay, lining it with resort hotels and motels. The bay is protected along its southern side by moles enclosing the harbour.

Timaru is the gateway to the MacKenzie Country, which is an immense upland basin named after a notorious sheep-stealer, a Highland shepherd named James McKenzie, who discovered it, and endeavoured to stock it with sheep from the flocks of the lowland station The Levels.

The northern entrance to the MacKenzie Country is via Burkes Pass, which climbs steeply through a narrow rift in the hills. Its official discoverer was one Michael John Burke, whose threefold monument consists of the pass itself, the pine plantations which line it, and the stone cairn with a plaque, which reads:

"To put on record that Michael John Burke, a graduate of Dublin University, and the first occupier of Raincliff Station, entered the pass known to the Maoris as Te Kopi Opihi, in 1855 – O ye who enter the portals of the MacKenzie to found homes, take the word of a child of the misty gorges and plant trees for your lives. So shall your mountain facings and river flats be preserved for evermore."

It is a remarkable bit of advice, coming from a man whose contemporaries' most usual activity was the burning off of bush to turn hillsides into pasture.

The MacKenzie Country does not look to be especially good grazing

The Church of the Good Shepherd, built of local stone, stands on the edge of
Lake Tekapo as a memorial to MacKenzie Country pioneers

Braemar Station, one of the great sheep runs of South Canterbury, lies amidst
the magnificent scenery of the eastern shore of Lake Pukaki

ground, yet it is. Merino sheep thrive there, evidently well able to cope with winter snows and the fierce 30° Celsius-plus heat of summer. It is a harsh-looking land, with comparatively few trees (in spite of Burke's solemn injunction), overlooked by eroding mountains, humped here and there with flat-topped, long hills.

There are more trees in evidence as you approach Lake Tekapo. Dark pines cluster about the lake's shore, with ranks of willow here and there. Near Tekapo village is a bare, grassy knoll overlooking the river, where stands the delightful little stone Church of the Good Shepherd, with its great picture window over its altar affording a splendid view down the lake.

The bridge over the river is, in fact, a dam to control storage for the Tekapo Hydro-Electric Power Station, regulating a flow of water generating some 20,000kw.

Lake Tekapo is the bed of an ancient glacier. It is fed by the Godley river and its tributary, the Macauley, and it drains out into the Waitaki river by way of the Tekapo. The lake is about 25 kilometres (15 miles) long, 5 kilometres (3 miles) in width at its widest point, and lies at an altitude of 707m (2321ft). Overlooking it is the hump of Mount John, at whose summit stands an observatory, sited here to take advantage of the clear mountain air and the record sunshine-and-clear-sky hours.

Across a tawny countryside of snowgrass, briar and wild gooseberries patched sparingly with pine shelter belts, lies Lake Pukaki, fed by the Tasman river which brings snow-water from the great Tasman and Hooker valleys. Pukaki is another glacier-bed lake, banked up behind hydro-electric works at its southern end, where the Pukaki river takes its outflow to swell the Waitaki

The road to Mount Cook and its famous hostelry, the Hermitage, runs around the western shore of the lake, and climbs over the hem of the Ben Ohau Range's skirts, into the Tasman valley.

Mount Cook is New Zealand's highest mountain, 3764m (12,349ft) high. Beneath it, the Tasman Glacier comes down, its lower reaches grey with gravel, although the ice beneath that grey mantle is about 122m (400ft) thick. Farther up, the dazzling reaches of the great ice-river are stained about its crevasses a glorious turquoise blue.

Mount Cook, of course, dominates all, soaring up above its mighty neighbours – sharp Mount Tasman, bulky Malte Brun, jagged La Perouse and lofty Mount Sefton. Mount Cook's Olympian height is almost matched by Mount Tasman's 3498m (11,475ft).

Sometimes, when the nor'wester starts to blow, a great mass of cloud covers the western side of the ranges, trapped by the high peaks yet still driven from behind by the hot north wind. From the air it provides an awesome spectacle, boiling like a pot of porridge, and eventually spilling in long slurps down the eastern side of the mountains.

There is skiing to be had hereabouts, and mountain climbing. But for the non-skier and non-climber, the principal attraction is the selection of interesting walks, surrounded by gigantic peaks; DuFaur, and Cadogan, reaching over 2743m (9000ft) into the sky, the supporters, as it were, of the heraldic splendour of the principal peaks.

These alpine heights are the haunt of the *kea*, the mountain parrot, who is fearless to the point of impudence, and who seems to have the appetite of an ostrich, for people camping in the mountain huts in this region dare not leave packs, food or even stout leather boots where he can get at them. He has been known to invade huts and tear mattresses

Mount Cook, the star of the great Mount Cook National Park, is called Aorangi by the Maoris, a name which means "Cloud Piercer"

and furnishings to shreds, perhaps in search of food or, more possibly, in a gratifying orgy of destruction.

South of Lake Pukaki is Lake Ohau, third of the major MacKenzie Country lakes, and smaller than the other two. It curves between the Ben Ohau and Barrier Ranges, fed by the Dobson river and its tributary, the Hopkins. It is drained by the Ohau river, a tributary of the Waitaki.

The southernmost village in the MacKenzie Country is Omarama, ("The Moonlit Place"), from which it is possible either to go down to Oamaru via Benmore and Aviemore, or on through the Lindis Pass to Central Otago and Queenstown.

The awesome ridge and sharp outline of Mount Tasman, one of the great peaks
to the north of Mount Cook

The tussock grasslands typical of the dry, eastern side of the Southern Alps, photographed here near Lindis Pass

Central Otago, the Southern Lakes and Fiordland

The Lindis Pass, dusty and hot in the summer, sometimes blocked with snow or floods in the winter, is a narrow road which twists between rounded, brown hills which look for all the world like the haphazard folds of a carelessly dropped, dun-coloured blanket. It follows the valley of the Lindis river, a narrow, sometimes willow-choked stream whose occasional flats, willow-shaded, are small oases in the stark countryside.

The road parts company with the river, separated from it by a long ridge, near the village of Tarras, a one-time goldmining town but now, as are many of the old gold towns of Central Otago, centre of a fruit-growing district where apricots are grown. West of Tarras lies Lake Wanaka, one of the two sources of the mighty Clutha river. Like all glacial lakes, it is long, and by comparison with its length, narrow. It twists and turns to form broad bays and interesting coves, and enwraps three islands, Ruby Island, Ram Island and Pigeon Island, which has a tiny lake of its own which, for no apparent reason, rises and falls.

The name of Lake Wanaka is a corruption of Oanaka, "The Place of Anaka", who was a prominent chief in the region. Its shores have not the sylvan beauty of the southern lakes, Te Anau and Manapouri, nor the mountain grandeur of Wakatipu, and its surrounding peaks are frequently

Above: This roofless cottage and a few similar ruins are all that is left of the gold-mining town of Bendigo in Central Otago
Opposite: The tints of early autumn mirrored in the still water of Glendhu Bay on Lake Wanaka

brown and barren-looking; but its beaches are often shady with maple and willow, and rowans lean over its water, smouldering colourfully in autumn, but cool and green and shady in summer. Wanaka is 45 kilometres (30 miles) long by 4.8 kilometres (3½ miles) wide at its widest point, with a total area of some 181 square kilometres (75 square miles). It is over 300m (1000ft) deep, and very cold. On its south-western shore is the Matukituki valley, where bush-patched pasture slopes down from the Harris Mountains, and through it brawls the Matukituki river, swelled by streams with such evocative names as Leaping Burn, and Boil-the-Billy Creek, which rush down from Black Peak's northern spurs and the flanks of Fog Peak. At the head of the valley, a sort of meeting place of the ranges, the Matukituki becomes a skein of gravelly waterways, as the river's east and west branches meet to become the river which, according to local legend, the Maoris called the White Destroyer.

East of Lake Wanaka is Lake Hawea, the other source of the Clutha. Hawea covers about 124 square kilometres (48 square miles), being some 35 kilometres (22 miles) long and about 8 kilometres (5 miles) wide across its broadest point. Its depth is about 335m (1100ft). A series of peaks rising over 1774m (5823ft) above the lake divides its southern end

from the northern end of Lake Wanaka, and the range which runs from Mount Grandview through Breast Hill to Dingle Peak forms its lofty eastern wall. A series of peaks rises between Hawea Flat and Lake Wanaka, and the road runs around the foot of this range, climbing around its northern end and dropping down to The Neck, and crossing from the western side of Lake Hawea to the eastern shore of Wanaka. From here it creeps along the steep sides of Wanaka's northern end until it reaches the Makarora valley, which leads to Haast Pass.

The Makarora valley runs through the northern end of Mount Aspiring National Park, an untamed and chilly paradise of glacial valleys, moraines and high, lost basins. Some appreciation of the country may be gained from the names given to its peaks by explorers and surveyors in the area – Mount Awful, Mount Dreadful, Mount Awkward, Mount Defiant, Sombre Peak, The Wart, Mount Dispute, Moonraker, Dragon Peak, Misty Peak, Foggy Top; and above it all soars Mount Aspiring, lifted up on four main ridges, the highest peak outside Mount Cook National Park.

Some 49km (30 miles) south of Lake Wanaka is Queenstown, once a mining town, perhaps the most sophisticated mining town of them all. It had electric light and gas in an era when other towns dotting the Central Otago highlands in those goldrush days – and, for that matter, other non-goldrush towns, now important and populous centres – were still collections of raupo and slab *whares*. Already, in those days, the beginnings of a more cultured concept of living were apparent in the fine stone-built library, and the Masonic Lodge, first in the area and the oldest stone building still being used for its original purpose anywhere in New Zealand.

Queenstown sits on the slope of an ancient moraine, about midway along the zig-zag line of Lake Wakatipu. In its mining heyday it was said of the lake that there were more ships plying on it than on the Mediterranean – an exaggeration, one suspects, but one which conjures up a reasonably accurate picture. There were indeed many craft where

Above: A panorama known to thousands of visitors to Queenstown: the view from the Peak Cableway of the town, Lake Wakatipu and the Remarkables
Opposite: Mount Aspiring dominates this scene in the Mount Aspiring National Park in Central Otago

Golden Terrace Mining Town, in Queenstown, is a recreation of a typical gold-mining town of the 1860s and 1870s

today there are mainly pleasure boats, tourist launches and the old steamship, *Earnslaw*. It, like Queenstown, is a survival, and the principal *raison d'être* for both is tourism. With the proliferation of hotels and motels of varying degrees of opulence, there is some danger of the truly historic town being swept away. Some insurance against this has been provided by the construction of Golden Terrace, a re-creation, not of Queenstown, particularly, but of a typical gold-rush town of the latter half of the nineteenth century. It is not merely a replica, but a collection of buildings and objects brought from other localities. There are shops, a mining company office, a bank, a furnished house and a smithy, smelling, as smithies always do, of a slightly acrid coke furnace, with that sour, metallic smell which seems to rise from the tub of cold water into which hot iron is plunged for cooling. Close by is a carpenter's shop, second most vital industry in such towns where everything in the way of machinery or shelter had to be constructed on the spot. There is a livery and bait stable, livery and bait signifying that you could hire a horse or equipage for travelling about the district, and that you could lodge your own horse there for care and feeding.

The Antrim Arms pub has been reconstructed there, as has the office of the now commercially defunct local newspaper, the *Wakatip* (sic) *Mail*, with its printing equipment.

On the shallow beginning of the slope behind the main street is the old schoolhouse, whose students must have been driven to distraction by the constant clamour of the nearby steam engine and stamping battery as it crushed the ore brought down from the mine whose entrance is higher up on the larch-grown slope.

"Wakatip", of course, is a careless contraction of the name of the lake, which is properly Whakatipua, a name which means "Trough of the

The sheer pinnacle of Mitre Peak dominates Milford Sound, rising from the deep waters of the fiord about half way along its southern edge

whose peak stabs 2095m (6873ft) into the blue sky. Even when you can't see them, even when clouds descend upon them and tear themselves to tatters upon those saw-tooth ridges, Clinton Canyon is beautiful, though perhaps in that mood a little awesome. Yet its floor is gentle, a place of green, glass-clear water, shaded by forests and glades of red beech, mighty *totara*, ribbonwood, a variety of ferns and, glorious in summer, flaming clusters of red *rata* blossom splashing the sombre, olive-drab of the native foliage. Shades of green and russet, the wet, green moss, the shafts of sunlight tinted as though they had slipped through the high, green clerestory windows of some vast cathedral, combine to work a quite unsubtle magic. Over a stretch of 2 or 3 kilometres (1½ to 2 miles) of the canyon, it broadens into a lightly-timbered river flat, a slightly

A cairn marks the Mackinnon Pass, discovered by Quintin Mackinnon, which made possible the formation of the Milford Track

inclined valley floor which steepens towards the point where the canyon walls close in again. In these narrows is the first overnight stop, the Pompolona Hut.

From there, the track goes on through the last narrowing kilometres of Clinton Canyon and climbs over the Mackinnon Pass. From the pass, with dark Clinton Canyon stretching away behind, and Olympian peaks all around, Arthur valley may be seen stretching away on to the mountain fastness, 600 vertical metres below. In that valley are the Quintin Huts, the second night's stopover, with, in their vicinity, Sutherland Falls, third highest in the world, spilling down vertical faces from Lake Quill in three mighty leaps, the first 288m (815ft), the second 229m (751ft) and the third 103m (338ft). The falls are half as high again as New York's Empire State Building, or, as one guide book puts it, four times the height of Sydney Harbour Bridge and more than five times the height of St Paul's Cathedral, London. When Lake Quill is in flood, the waters curve out beyond the rocky ledges in a single leap of 620m (1904ft).

The track ends with the crossing of Lake Ada, or, if preferred, a scenic walk around it, past Giant Gate Falls, to Doughboy Landing in Milford Sound itself.

South of Lake Te Anau is Lake Manapouri. Manapouri was originally – and slightly libellously – named Roto-ua by the high chief Rakaehautu over 1100 years ago. The name means "Rainy Lake". Sometime later, nobody knows quite when, it was given the rather more commonplace name of Moturau, "Many Islands", for obvious reasons. Its present name is a corruption of Manawapouri, which means "Sorrowing Heart". According to legend, it was formed by the tears of two heartbroken sisters, Motuau and Koronae. Considering that its depth is about 440m (1445ft), which puts the lake bottom a good 266m (872ft) below sea level, making it the deepest lake in New Zealand, they must have had a really good cry.

Certainly it is the most beautiful lake in this land of handsome lakes. Its deep coves, its North, South and West Arms, its thirty-six islands, the glorious forest which comes down from the mountains to gaze at its

The Sutherland Falls, the highest of several falls in Milford Sound, are named
after the Scotsman, Donald Sutherland, who discovered them

reflection in the still waters, or to stand admiringly around the small,
sandy beaches, give it a calm beauty that is felt as well as seen. The main
Manapouri settlement is Pearl Harbour, situated at the lake's outlet,
where the Lower Waiau river flows out of the lake and down a narrow
valley which runs south-east clear to Foveaux Strait.

In West Arm beneath Leaning Peak is the control building for the
hydro-electric power generating plant which, taking advantage of the
lake's height above sea level, taps off its water through vast penstocks
pierced through the bowels of the mountains to spill out into Doubtful
Sound, a somewhat Milford-like fiord opening into the Tasman Sea. Tour
buses take sightseers over the Wilmot Pass to Deep Cove in Doubtful
Sound, an awe-inspiring journey with overtones of Peer Gynt.

Dunedin, the South Otago
Coast and Stewart Island

Although not every citizen of Dunedin cares for the city's image of "Scottishness", it is hard to escape from it. Dunedin seems to be a happy survival of much that is finest and best in Scottish culture. Critics of such a view are afraid that it freezes Dunedin into the Victorian era, inhibits the go-ahead spirit of the city, and makes cultural growth impossible.

Nevertheless, Dunedin is indubitably, indomitably Scottish. It was founded by Scottish Free Church immigrants in 1848, and was even to have been called New Edinburgh; but on a happy inspiration it was given the Celtic form of the name.

Dunedin is superficially Victorian, having sensibly retained the cream of its Victorian heritage. It has an air of dependable solidity, and seems to have grown out of its own craggy landscape in Victorian times, with the result that it is a comfortable, hill-guarded city, tilted to catch the sun. It has a solid, civilised grandeur, reminding today's brasher world that its base is solid, architecturally founded on rock, economically based on the gold discoveries of the hinterland. For a considerable time it was the largest city in New Zealand, and still, when New Zealanders are asked to name their four principal cities, they automatically list Auckland, Wellington, Christchurch and Dunedin. In the matter of size, Dunedin is no longer even fourth; but it has been, almost from the beginning, a place of handsome mansions and public and ecclesiastical buildings and fine amenities. It was so when northern towns were collections of shanties.

It is still, perhaps, the pleasantest of all New Zealand cities in which to live, and could have some justification in claiming to be the country's cultural heart, having produced some of New Zealand's most prestigious

Above: Considered by many to be the finest church in New Zealand, Dunedin's
Presbyterian First Church was designed by a Scot. R. A. Lawson
Opposite: The University of Otago's Clock Tower has gazed down on succeeding
generations of students since 1878

writers, artists and scholars. Almost from its beginning it has been a
university town, and town and university do not co-exist in uneasy peace
as is the case in most other university towns in New Zealand, but seem to
be proudly and mutually supportive. Indeed, a large area of the city's
northern quarter comprises the University of Otago's campus.

Dunedin's situation (like Rome, on seven hills) is pleasant, and it
enjoys a climate which is cooler than that of most northern cities, to be
sure, yet one which is mild and moderate.

There is a self-confidence in its architecture which is calmly assured
rather than brashly assertive. That can be seen in its railway station,
which looks more like a House of Parliament, all granite solidity and tile-
lined opulence; in its educational establishments with all the consequence
of baronial castles; in its elegant Victorian and Edwardian mansions, still
as gracious as they were, and often more comfortable and convenient than
many a modern home – and still, as often as not, occupied by the
descendants of the families for whom they were built.

The heart of Dunedin is the Octagon, a small, pleasant, terraced
green in the commercial centre of the city. It is presided over by the
Town Hall and, oddly enough in this Presbyterian city, the Anglican
Cathedral Church of St Paul. There is a sort of outer Octagon (which is
more pronouncedly octagonal), known as Moray Place, on the southern
side of which is First Church, an airily soaring Gothic Revival church in
dressed Oamaru stone, a likely contender for the title of the finest Gothic
Revival church in New Zealand – or perhaps anywhere. It has an
exuberance about it which they would have understood and approved of

A piece of England in Dunedin: the study at Olveston, designed by an English
architect in consciously English styles for businessman, David Theomin

in the Middle Ages, and which stops on the right side of flamboyance.
First Church was built at the instigation of the settlers' first minister, the
Rev. Thomas Burns, nephew of the great Robbie Burns, that forthright
poet whose statue stands – or sits – in the Octagon. The church was
designed by R.A. Lawson, a young architect then in his early twenties,
who also designed the very fine Knox Church, sitting on its awkward site
on George Street.

Most opulent of all the mansions is Olveston, designed by Sir Ernest
George, one of England's greatest domestic architects in the Edwardian
period. Designed in the Jacobean style, many of its parts were shipped out
from England. It was to be a "modern" house, built to provide the
greatest degree of luxury and comfort that human ingenuity could con-
trive, and it still stands head and shoulders above most modern homes in
that regard. Filled with art treasures, it is open to the public, by
appointment, having been given to the city by the last surviving daughter
of Mr D.E. Theomin, for whom it was built.

Across the harbour lies the Otago Peninsula. It does not, like
Canterbury's Banks Peninsula, stick out into the Pacific Ocean like a rude
Cockney thumb, but lies alongside the long, narrow harbour, forming its
eastern wall. From the peninsula's high, hill roads, the harbour looks like
a Scottish loch, an impression heightened by small (by New Zealand
standards) farms with drystone fences and stone buildings. From its castle-
crowned heights to its dreaming, old-fashioned and sometimes cheerfully
informal harbourside settlements, it is a place of charming and determined
anachronisms. The harbourside road itself is a relic of the days when a
sentence of hard labour could still be handed out by an outraged judge. It
was built by convict labour under the supervision of an engineer whose

Close to the city of Dunedin, yet totally rural, the Otago Peninsula also has much to interest the naturalist, including an important albatross colony

admirably simple instructions were "Stay with the high-tide mark".

Not quite farthest out is Portobello, where a marine biology station maintains an interesting aquarium displaying common food fish, and a *tuatara*, that survivor from the age of dinosaurs. He remains absolutely motionless for hours at a time, perhaps dreaming of the days when his close relatives owned the earth, or hearing – and maybe seeing with that vestigial third eye – as in a dream in his little, sculpted, dinosaur head, their mighty tramp and thunder.

Around the next deep bay and over a shoulder of a hill is the Maori settlement of Otakou, from which this Province got its name. It was the home of the chief Taiaroa, who signed the Treaty of Waitangi on behalf of the Southern Tribes. His direct descendant, also Taiaroa, lives here now.

The settlement possesses a Maori church and a school, odd mixtures of European and traditional Maori building. Even the gatepost carving, which is very fine, has been carried out in concrete rather than in wood, though it is painted as wood always was, with *kokowai* – red ochre.

Otago, which many New Zealanders grew up believing was a good Scottish word, wasn't. It was merely what the original settlers made of Otakou. (The same obvious difficulty posed by Maori to the Gaelic tongue is evident all over the province. The great hump of hill which the main road climbs on its way north from Dunedin, the Kilmog, than which nothing could sound more Scottish, should really be *Kirimoko*, the name of a shrub which grows profusely hereabouts; and the gorge through which one drives to reach Queenstown, and the river which flows through it, is called K'warrah, even though it is spelt correctly, as Kawarau.)

On Taiaroa Head is the only place in the world where the albatross nests close to human habitation. The area has been fenced off to protect

The grand folly of a politician; Larnach's Castle was built by the Hon. William Larnach so that his aristocratic French wife might be housed in suitable style

the colony, which is somewhat precarious. These magnificent birds live to 40 to 70 years old, and are very slow to establish themselves as a colony. This one established itself in 1920, and the first successful rearing of a chick did not occur till 1938, since when some 85 chicks have reached maturity. Standing 75cm (29 inches) high they, have a wingspan of some 3.2m (10½ft), and can weigh up to 10kg (20lb). They are a magnificent sight as they wheel and soar near the lighthouse on the head.

From Portobello – named after the Scottish Portobello, which itself was named after the Spanish Porto Bello of the Panama Isthmus, sacked by the British in 1793 – a road climbs up to the top of the peninsula, past the ancient volcanic plug known as Harbour Cone, to Larnach's Castle, which might not, by architectural definition, be a true castle, but which is best described as a fortified manor. It was built in the 1870s by the Hon. W.J.M. Larnach, a Member of Parliament and a man of considerable political strength and influence. He married a daughter of the Duc de Guise, Pretender to the French Throne, and evidently decided that she must have a home which befitted her station in life. Plans were drawn up overseas, and the building was supervised by that R.A. Lawson who designed First Church. Workmen and many materials were imported from overseas. Its superb plaster ceilings are the work of Venetian plasterers, and the wonderful wood carving was done by a man named Phillip Godfrey, using practically every building and joining wood in the world, much of it quite untypical of its type. There are mahogany beams, wonderful ceilings of English oak with dark mahogany carvings in full relief. There is a ballroom, built as a present for a favourite daughter, for

whom Larnach also peopled the gardens with figures described in some guide leaflets as "gnomes", but which are undoubtedly characters from *Alice in Wonderland*, modelled after the drawings of Sir John Tenniel. Surprisingly – and, in some respects, Scottishly – in one who conceived such a romantic fantasy, Larnach called it "The Camp", a name which he had set in mosaic on the foyer floor.

Larnach came to a sad end. Beset by financial and family troubles, he shot himself in his room in Parliament Buildings in Wellington in 1898. His tomb, however, left an unmistakable impression of both his stature and his personality. It stands in Dunedin's old Northern Cemetery, a scaled-down copy of First Church, no less!

The South Otago Coast

South of Dunedin, the coastline runs down in a series of swoops, with high hills never very far from the sea. About 18 kilometres (12 miles) south of the city, on the edge of a countryside of rolling hills and bush-filled valleys, Brighton stands on a low shelf, its outermost houses strung out along a road which is hidden from the sea by lupin-covered sandhills. The older part of the township clusters around the estuary of the Otokia river. It was named after the popular English resort, in the hope that it would become equally popular, and it certainly attracted Dunedinites as a good place for a summer holiday, but the beaches north and south proved dangerous for swimming, which somewhat limited its appeal.

This whole coast is prone to dangerous tidal and current rips, but there are, spaced out along it, stretches protected by reef and headland

213

which divert the fierce currents and enclose attractive, gently shelving and safe curves of golden sand.

South of Brighton is Taieri Mouth, crouching beneath a huge, bush-patched hill, a picturesque, rather un-New Zealand fishing village whose colourful fishing boats are tied up alongside a few jetties precariously set on spindly piling. It could hardly be called an enclosed or landlocked harbour, but it is sheltered by Taieri Island, a small isle whose name was bestowed by Europeans, this being the mouth of the Taieri river. The Maoris called it Moturata, Rata Island, possibly because it was believed to mark the northern limit of the southern species of *rata*.

Eighty-two kilometres (51 miles) south of Dunedin is the town of Balclutha, so called because it sits astride the mighty Balclutha river; and south of Balclutha is some of the most spectacular coastline on this southern coast, a region of cruel promontories and long, empty beaches backed by sombrely splendid forest, cliffs, caves and estuaries. It is a region where whales may sometimes be seen spouting at no great distance offshore, where penguins and seals are fairly commonplace, and where there are unspoiled tracts of forest and one of the loveliest waterfalls in the country.

A little to the south of Kaka Point, Nugget Point reaches out into the sea, a razor-backed headland whose shoreward flanks are covered with forest trees which have been dwarfed and shaped by the sea winds to form a pattern of whorls and streaks and eddies. There is a lighthouse on the point, below which seals may be seen basking on the hillside grass, or on narrow ledges incomprehensibly high above the water, on the pinnacles of rock known as the Nuggets, from which the point takes its name.

Farther south still is the area known as the Catlins, where some of the loveliest, most varied scenery in the entire South Island may be seen.

The Catlins countryside about the principal township, the tiny hamlet of Owaka, which means "The Place of Canoes", is green and well-favoured, with high, bush-clad hills and deep, sheltered valleys. A warm ocean current flows past golden beaches, never varying in temperature by more than about 3°C, throughout the year. From August through September and October, *rata* and clematis star and paint the dark forest.

This was timber milling country in the early days. The main timber trees hereabouts are *kahikitea*, *rimu* and *matai*, and in the days when timber milling was at its height, and flat-bottomed scows crowded into that broad stretch of the Catlins river still known as Catlins Lake, twenty-six large mills operated. As the bush was cleared, small farms sprang up like mushrooms, and little settlements grew up, loose collections of small farmsteads with their schools, churches and stores. But the land, though fertile, is heavy, and once the timber mills began to diminish in number, and there was no longer such a large and ready market for milk, meat, butter and vegetables, the economics of small-farming became sticky, and the titanic labour needed to farm that heavy countryside no longer returned a decent living. Neighbour sold out to marginally more successful neighbour, and small farms gradually became big farms, which in turn became great farms. Today, set in bush-patched valleys and on hillsides, there still stand occasional derelict churches, empty little schools and mouldering farmhouses, some of which are little gems of Victorian colonial domestic architecture with their simple design, steep roofs and gable windows.

But the big farms prosper. This area is, for some blessed reason, singularly free of livestock diseases, the climate is moderate, and the

A fine attraction in the Catlins district, the Purakaunui Falls flow gracefully over terraces in the bush-edged Purakaunui river

timber millers had sufficient foresight to leave untouched large stands of timber which today provide shelter and hold the hillsides together, happily free from the erosion which has damaged most areas of New Zealand hill country which was stripped of forest and sown in grass.

A road still wanders through the forested hills, hiding such scenic gems as the Purakaunui Falls. Happily, the local people have rescued such delightful scenes from obscurity, building tracks into them, signposting them at the roadsides, and even constructing ample car parks.

The Purakaunui Falls tumble down a steep hillside over three main steps of rock, dividing on their bottom leap into an arrangement of tiered minor cataracts. The water does not fall into a great basin, but on to a channelled shelf of rock, from which it gurgles and chuckles away through a glade of moss-festooned trees.

From the top of Florence Hill there is a panoramic view of one of the finest seascapes on this notably glamorous coast. Tautuku Bay, a perfect 3.5-kilometre (2½-mile) crescent of golden sand, stretches away to where the Tautuku Peninsula reaches out, low, green and tree-patched, with its scatter of small holiday baches and farm buildings, into the blue Pacific.

Cars may drive along the firm, yellow sand, but the shallow Tahakopa

river, fanning out broadly across the beach, is still deep enough to bar the
way to the peninsula, which can, however, be reached on foot at low
tide, or by one of the high-wheeled tractors the crib owners keep for the
purpose.

The Tautuku Peninsula is indented with tiny, secluded coves, above
which rise green and grassy slopes dotted with shady groves. It slopes
gently down to the mainland, but presents to the sea ramparts and
pinnacles of lumpy conglomerate which contains rubies, sapphires and
gold – not, alas, in paying quantities or sizes. Once the site of a whaling
station, the peninsula once had gardens, maintained to provide fresh
vegetables for the crews; and a deep fissure on the southern flank of the
isthmus is still known as Whalers' Garden.

South of Tautuku Bay, the name of which means "Bend", probably a
reference to the symmetrical curve of the beach, is Waipati Beach, where
there are eleven lofty caverns in the seaside cliffs, known as Cathedral
Caves, great, echoing tunnels, where ferns grow astonishingly head down
from the domed roof, and the rock walls are painted with the glistening
reds and greens of algae and leafed plants. The rocky cliffs have interesting stratification, including coal seams.

217

The children's fountain, surrounded by bronze statues of animals, in Queen's Park, Invercargill

Invercargill and Bluff

Invercargill, New Zealand's southernmost city, sits on the banks of the Waihopai river, near where it runs into the New River Estuary. An attractive city, its urban population is about 50,000. Invercargill is a place of broad, well-planned streets. Like Christchurch, it is flat, and – also like Christchurch – is well endowed with parks and reserves, about 5,600ha (14,000 acres) in all, about 260ha (500 acres) of which are within the urban boundaries. The town was planned – again, like Christchurch – four-square, with broad thoroughfares that are not overtaxed even by today's traffic, and were named after Scottish rivers – Dee, Forth, Esk, Tay and others – none of your Maori nomenclature nonsense for the Chief Surveyor of Otago Province! – and the city was named after Captain Cargill, Superintendent of Otago Province, at the suggestion of Governor Gore-Browne. It became a borough in 1871, a city in 1930.

The city itself is clean and open, with many fine homes, and has at its back door the magnificent sandy Oreti Beach. In the city proper, the beautiful heart is Queens Park, 64ha (160 acres) of gardens, lawns and trees, a sunken rose garden, a splendid rhododendron walk and a fine wildlife sanctuary. Near its entrance is a small "transplanted" section of a petrified forest, stumps mostly, of saplings, some larger trees and a couple of fallen trees.

Anderson Park, which is outside the city, is an estate and homestead bequeathed to the city by Sir Robert and Lady Anderson. Now an art gallery, the mansion is set at the head of verdant lawns which sweep down, dotted with garden plots and screened from the workaday driveway by climbing roses, to a lily-covered water where ducks raise their broods, leading them as soon as possible up to the house, to beg for food.

The house backs on to native bush, and is a very fine, simple

A fishing boat at Bluff, where more fish and shellfish, especially the famous
Foveaux Strait oysters, are landed than at any other New Zealand port

Sunset at Red Sand Cove – a remote and peaceful spot on the ragged coast of Stewart Island

Georgian-style structure, white and clean but of good design. When its floors were carpeted and its fires lit, and people were living their lives in it, it must have been warmly gracious. Today there are odds and ends of furniture in its rooms, its fireplaces are cold, and it has no heartbeat – but it does contain some beautiful works of art.

Behind it, backing shyly into the shadow of the bush, is a carved Maori house. It has the appearance of a meeting house, but is far too small for that. It might be a *whare puni*, a sleeping house, but it is unusual for such a building to be so ornate. Probably it was specially built for use

as a summer house, the carving commissioned for the purpose. Whatever its origin, its carving is worth seeing.

The land between Invercargill and Bluff, southernmost port in New Zealand, is flat and scrubby and inclined to swampiness. The road skirts the New River estuary for a kilometre or so, then sidles across the neck of land which separates the estuary from the landlocked harbour of Bluff.

Bluff is the home port of the oyster fleet, which dredges Foveaux Strait for oysters, harvesting over 115,000 sacks annually. A 29ha (72-acre) island has been reclaimed from the harbour to provide extra berthage for coastal, overseas and what is anachronistically described as inter-colonial shipping between New Zealand and Australia. There are additional berths across at Tiwai Point, serving the aluminium smelter.

From Bluff's 237m (778ft) summit, wonderful panoramic views are obtained of Bluff itself, of Ruapuke Island, Dog Island and the whole sweep of coastline westward to the Fiordland mountains and, dark and high, across some 30 kilometres (20 miles) of frequently turbulent water, Stewart Island.

Stewart Island

Amongst the many tales and legends concerning the origins of New Zealand is the all-embracing myth concerning the demi-god, Maui, who set sail with his brothers in a vast canoe, on a fishing expedition. They caught the North Island, still known as *Te Ika a Maui*, "Maui's Fish" (though how a people without maps perceived the possibility of the tale from the overall shape of the North Island is a mystery in itself). The South Island, of course, was the canoe, *Te Waka a Maui*, and Stewart Island was *Te Punga o te Waka a Maui*, "The Anchor Stone of Maui's Canoe".

In the course of time the last named received another name, *Rakiura*, "The Glowing Sky", so called, it is said, because of the wonderful sunsets seen from it, though one might reasonably suspect that the Aurora Australis, visible from the island in winter, had rather more to do with it. In any case, it was eventually called by the less glamorous name of Stewart Island, after the First Officer of the ship *Pegasus*, who first surveyed it in 1809.

Captain Cook knew of it, naturally; but he, who called Banks Peninsula an island, wrote that ". . . when I came to lay it down on paper from the several bearings I had taken it appeared that there was little reason to suppose it an Island. On the contrary I hardly have a doubt but what it joins to and makes a part of the mainland." And if anyone feels like scoffing at a man who could miss spotting thirty-odd kilometres of water and imagine that it was land, please remember that he was viewing it from the quarterdeck of a small ex-collier which was prudently keeping its distance in this moody, rough sea – as who wouldn't? This is one of the most turbulent stretches of water in the world.

Stewart Island, which the overwhelming majority of New Zealanders never see, and therefore imagine to be a hump of bush-covered rock a little way off the southern coast, actually sprawls over an area of about 1746 square kilometres (670 square miles). It is partially, even largely, bush clad, but manages to include some surprisingly large tussock plains and moors, several small lakes, navigable rivers and some respectably-sized mountains, of which Mount Anglem, the highest, reaches 975m (3200ft). The next tallest, Mount Rakaehua, is 676m (2217ft) high.

Stewart Island has been mined for tin and gold, and has, in its day, had timber mills and flax mills; but these industries have long since gone. The Maoris, too, have largely left it, having sold it in 1864 for £6000; but its inhabitants today include descendants of important Maori families as well as a somewhat larger proportion of *Pakeha*. Most of them are fisherfolk, with a storekeeper, an hotel proprietor, some boarding house

Whale Bay, like many other bays around Stewart Island's indented coast, is
seldom visited

proprietors and a farmer or two. Most of them live in the tiny township of
Oban, the island's only town, which is a cluster of houses, churches, a
pub, a school, a store and a museum at the head of Halfmoon Bay. The
sea laps at the little village's feet, the forest crowds down at its back, and
the roads run out for only a kilometre or two on either side of it, thin
arms resting on rocky, forested spurs.

Within walking distance of Oban are beautiful beaches – the golden,
clean sands of Bathing Beach and Butterfield Bay, and the silvery sand of
Horseshoe Bay, which is frequently littered with a scarlet seaweed, and
where charming little cottages with roses around their doors squat serenely
at the foot of a huge, dark, forested hill.

The interior of the island is for experienced and properly equipped
hunters and trampers, but launch trips are available which visit the
offshore islands, and even explore the southern coastline. Ulva Island and
Iona Island are ringed with bays and coves of haunting beauty. They are
uninhabited, and the native birds in the still, gorgeous forest are remarkably unafraid and even friendly.

There are short walks on the southern side of Oban, around the shores
of Paterson Inlet, a mighty gash which reaches into the very heart of the
island. Golden Bay, Wheelers Beach, Thule Bay, Vaila Voe, evocatively-
named localities, lie along a delightful bush walk through bird-haunted
forest where *kiwis* are sometimes seen in broad daylight, even though they
are, generally, of nocturnal habit, and where, in season, *kakas*, the native
bush parrots, become tipsy on nectar from native flowers and, it is said,
may often be heard late at night, giving fruity, inebriated chuckles.
Robins and fantails accompany strollers in this lovely region, and jewel-
bright kingfishers dive for their prey in idyllic coves.

The island may be reached by air or by ferry, the latter often being a
somewhat bumpy, two-hour trip across this notoriously rough stretch of
water. Yet it is a more interesting trip than the aircraft flight, passing
fishing boats and many small islands, including Dog Island, on which
stands New Zealand's southernmost lighthouse, and the Mutton Bird

Paterson Inlet, being near Oban, the only settlement on Stewart Island, shows more signs of habitation than many parts of the island

Islands, from which come another New Zealand delicacy, the mutton bird, which is the young of the Sooty Shearwater. It is the exclusive right of the Maoris to hunt these creatures, although, to be honest, there is little enough hunting involved. They nest in hollows and holes in the rocky faces of offshore islands, and are plucked out with leather-gloved hands, to be killed, smoked and eaten. Highly fancied by many people, they are nevertheless an acquired taste; being oily, not especially inviting to look at, and tasting not unlike kippers.

223

Sheep grazing on the summer pastures of the Makarora valley north of Lake Wanaka on the road up to the Haast Pass

Westland, Buller and
the Nelson Lakes

Native bush at Haast Pass, which was used by the Maoris as a greenstone route
centuries before it was "discovered" by Europeans

The Makarora valley, which stretches northwards from the head of Lake
Wanaka, along the eastern edge of Mount Aspiring National Park, is a
long series of river flats with intriguing names such as Millionaire Flat,
where, in the middle 1930s, a millionaire built a luxury resort with
chalet-type accommodation, swimming pool and every pleasant amenity,
from which he offered safari trips into the magnificent mountain wilderness. The scheme was ahead of its time, coming as it did at the tail-end
of the great Slump, in a country where very few people were particularly
wealthy. Few people came, and eventually the owner of the place just
packed up and moved out. No sign remains to show it was ever there.

Presently the road begins to climb into the Haast Pass sector of Mount
Aspiring National Park, where the Makarora river, not yet the braided,
gravel-choked complex of waterways that it becomes farther down the
valley, meanders pleasantly through forest.

The forest is glorious, a bird-loud place, garrulous with the chatter of
streams as they burble over clean, moss-lined beds; and it is punctuated
with enchanting glades, such as Camerons Flat, from which may be
obtained a first glimpse of the dominating peak in this area, the white
triple crown of Mount Brewster. The grade now begins to steepen as it
runs up to Haast Pass summit, at an altitude of 562m (1847ft).

The road dips down to Blue Duck Flat, from which is obtained a
much finer view of Mount Brewster and the Brewster Glacier, with

226

The Gates of Haast, where the Haast river drops from its level valley into a
steep gorge, with towering vertical walls

The view at Knights Point, where a plaque records the opening in 1965 of the final stretch of the Haast Pass route, a century after the road was first mooted

Fantail Falls glinting away through the trees. The Park authorities have placed here (and at other points of interest along the road) an indicator plate of stainless steel, engraved with a picture of the surrounding countryside, identifying the peaks and presenting a brief story on the native bird and plant life in the vicinity.

Blue Duck Flat is named – it seems obvious – after the blue duck, (*Hymenolaimus malacorhynchos*), one of New Zealand's four native species of duck, recognisable, if they happen to be about, by the oddly formed bill, with its flexible black membrane along each side, and by the blue-grey plumage and the chestnut spotting on breast and flanks.

From Blue Duck Flat, the road descends steeply to Gates of Haast bridge, slipping down to it between the mountain spurs. It is especially steep in the vicinity of the confluence of the Wills and Haast rivers. Gates of Haast bridge is a Callander-Hamilton bridge, opened in 1961 as a replacement for the original bridge, whose abutments may be seen upstream. It was a concrete structure, carried away in 1957 by a flood, and by those massive, house-sized boulders which choke the streambed.

Mount Brewster rises up from the eastern side of Gates of Haast, a splendid peak of the Main Divide, just under 2518m (8261ft), high enough to prevent the sun from reaching the road surface throughout winter, which makes this road treacherous with ice.

The Haast river hereabouts is a tumultuous rush of wild water, bashing its way around immense boulders and sluicing past mighty rock walls. This is almost unbelievably beautiful country, not merely wild but primeval.

The road comes down to the valley through which the Haast river, swelled now by the Clarke and Landsborough rivers, flows powerfully across vast river flats down to the sea. The road crosses it at no great distance from the Tasman Sea coast, and begins to run across forested sand dunes and a number of swamps, which may sound dreary but are, in reality, quite beautiful. Swift and powerful streams rush down from the mountain heights, streams with fascinating and quite undignified names bestowed on them by gold miners of a past era and by the men who made this road, names like Ship Creek, Bullock Creek, Breccia Creek, and features called Sardine Terrace, Epitaph Cutting and Knights Point.

Ship Creek is so named because it is sometimes possible to see, when the tide is out, the remains of a ship protruding from the sand near the mouth of the creek. It is believed to be the 2284-ton *Schomberg*, the biggest wooden ship ever launched, it is said, from a British shipyard. She was wrecked off Tasmania in December 1855, and how her remains finished up on this wild coast is something of a mystery.

Knights Point was named after a black Labrador dog, pet of one of the road's surveyors, whose head the rocky bluff is said to resemble.

Along this stretch of the way, the character of the coast changes. Gone are the windswept, desolate beaches. Now there are lofty cliffs and little secret coves, where the beach is sandy and undisturbed, and there are slim needles of rock rising from the sea, where the seals may be seen basking. The cliffs are shot with pink colourings in the rock, and deep red moss flourishes on the roadside banks.

The character of the country changes again, briefly, as it comes down from the high coastal bluffs to the bush-patched flats of the Moeraki river; and suddenly, there is Lake Moeraki, calm and lovely, sheltered from the ruffling breezes by a screen of tall timber.

There is a succession of lovely little lakes from here on; Lake Paringa, whose name is said to mean "Valley of Darkness", though this is almost

certainly a mistranslation. Pari-nga is "High Tide", or "Flowing Tide", and this is the most likely meaning of the lake's name, for it is curved and narrow, fed by Windbag Creek, and with only one outflow. In times of flood, the whole lake flows, and it seems to be just a wider stretch of the stream, running quickly down to the sea.

The Paringa valley is a sort of frontier farming area, where tracts of forest have been cleared, and sheep and cattle now graze the new, rough grassland. This is farming as the pioneers knew it over a century ago, except that axe and firestick have been supplanted by bulldozer and chain saw. But the homesteads still tend to be simple dwellings of the kind the pioneers built. Here and there a more permanent-looking, more substantial homestead has been erected, but by and large it is primitive-looking country where, as it was in pioneer times, life is a constant struggle, not only to clear land, but also to keep it cleared in these regions where some 4500mm (180inches) of rain falls annually, and growth is prolific.

But it is still beautiful country. The road is good, an elevated ribbon of tarseal running across swamp and through forest. There is so much beauty to see, so many deliciously peaceful little dells, sheltered by thick forest from the Tasman Sea breezes, with small clusters of beehives leaning this way and that, like crazy leprechaun-sized white apartment blocks rising out of the rank grass and bracken.

The road goes on, now quite close to the sea, now swinging away from it, now across river flats, now through forest. It crosses the Jacobs river, a tiny settlement named after the Maori ferryman in the 1880s, and the Karangarua river, at whose bridge a signpost marks the start of a walking track over the Copland Pass in the high Alps, to the Hermitage,

Above The red of the rata flower splashes the dark green of the bush with colour in the valley of the Fox river
Opposite: Lake Moeraki, near the coast north of Knights Point, is a trout fisherman's paradise, with great scenic beauty matched by good catches

Mount Cook. Some trampers do not go all the way to Mount Cook, but follow the Karangarua river through some glorious country to Welcome Flat, where there is hut accommodation for overnight stays. There are hot springs hereabouts, and one of life's most sublime experiences must be to lie luxuriating in the hot water, watching the mighty snow avalanches crashing down from the surrounding, safely distant peaks.

Just north of Sullivans Creek is the boundary of Westland National Park, which stretches from the Tasman Sea to the Main Divide, and encloses some 350,000ha (1350 square miles) of mountain and bush scenery.

Quite suddenly, the road crosses the Cook river and, 4 kilometres (2 miles) farther on, the Fox river, milky with "rock flour", which is rock ground from the mountainsides by the great icefall of the Fox Glacier.

Fox Glacier

Fox Glacier township is built upon an ancient moraine. It stands, therefore, on rising ground with dense forest at its back and the mountains rising, almost leaning, over it. From its western side, the harsh farmland stretches away, fertile river flats marching with the Cook river towards the sea but, unlike the river, intercepted by a lofty, forested complex of spurs terminating in a vast swamp. Beyond these spurs lies Gillespies Beach, and nestling within their lower branches repose two gem-like little lakes. East of the township is Fox Glacier itself, one of the finest spectacles in New Zealand, hemmed in by spurs, ridges and peaks, forest and rock face, wherein lies a recreation area which is, with that of Franz Josef 30 kilometres (20 miles) to the north, unique in New Zealand.

The terminus of the Fox Glacier. The glacier, which has retreated
2.4 kilometres (1½ miles) in the past 70 years, flows 1.5m (5ft) per day

Cne of the great characters of the Southern Alps, *Nestcr notabilis*, the *kea* or mountain parrot

The approach road to the glacier runs between stands of *rata* and *kamahi* for some 5 kilometres (3 miles), a delightful, all-weather route which, nevertheless, has some surprises. It curves around ancient moraines, and across gravelly terrain founded on dead ice, which has a nasty habit of melting in patches and leaving sudden potholes. Its final stretch is largely a cleared, adequately flattened area over debris which has fallen from crumbling mountainsides no longer supported by the glacial ice which, after advances in about 1600 and again in 1750, has retreated a considerable distance.

The car park at the end of the road is the haunt of small flocks of *kea*, that avian clown of the Southern Alps, who is apt to settle curiously on parked vehicles, to walk over their roofs, to fiddle interestedly with windscreen wipers and to announce his finds with raucous parrot cries. The *kea* (native mountain parrot) is predominantly green in colour, with a bright orange-red patch on the under-surface of each wing. He is a highly intelligent bird, playful, insatiably inquisitive and, like Jerome K. Jerome's fox terrier, is often suspected of having about twice as much original sin in him as other birds. His scientific name is *Nestor notabilis*, which may sound like the name of an American High Court judge, but the bird is a cheerful villain, capable of property vandalism which makes the efforts of travelling sports teams seem trivial by comparison.

The face of the glacier, or that portion of it which is not buried in the terminal moraine, is a jagged tumble of ice, part of it arching over a big

Visitors make a close inspection of the great river of ice that is the 15 kilometres
(9 miles) long Fox Glacier

ice-cave from which issues the Fox river, a tributary of the Cook. The water is not, as might be suspected, ice-melt, but comes from a spring high up in the mountains, tunnelling its way irresistibly under the ice. It rushes out from the ice-cave, snowy with powdered rock, across a river flat, curving here and there around a mighty rubble of mountain-wall debris. The riverbed and the valley floor actually sit on "dead" ice, stationary ice left behind in the glacier's slow retreat, filling a valley of unknown depth. It has been sounded to a depth of over 300m (1000ft) without positively reaching valley bottom.

The visible, "living" ice is a pristine white on the surface except where, here and there, it has been soiled by falls of rubble; but when looked directly into, it reveals depths of an attractive turquoise shade.

The glacier descends from the great snowfields beneath some of the highest peaks of the Southern Alps, a slightly zig-zagging course of nearly 15 kilometres (9 miles), dropping 300m (1000ft) per mile.

There are walks to numerous lookout points from which the glacier can be seen to advantage, and over which the course of earlier advances of the glacier may be traced by the varying stages of forest regeneration. Mount Fox, Cone Rock, Fox Chalet Outlook, High Valley Lookout, the Staircase, and Craig Peak all offer glorious views of this awesome ice river; and a ramble known as Moraine Walk, which can be done in twenty to thirty minutes, shows the history of the glacier as no other walk does, revealing, amongst other signs of a great foray towards the sea in 1600 or thereabouts, a ridge of "push" moraine, a tumbled mass of earth, rocks and forest trees which the Fox Glacier shoved ahead of itself with irresistible force, like a gargantuan bulldozer.

The forest abounds in interesting plant life, including stands of *rata*, mighty giants whose massive branches are festooned with a fantastic variety of orchids and tufted with perching plants. In one area, *rata* and *kamahi* are locked together in a life-and-death struggle, a battle of the Titans in which the *rata* has surrounded the trunk of the *kamahi* with its roots – a botanical irony, since both plants start life as parasites.

The jumble of ridges and spurs which lies between the township and Gillespies Beach encloses, on its eastern side, the exquisite Lake Matheson, once a huge block of "dead" ice, and now a mirror-still expanse of water, surrounded by forest and reflecting the mountain peaks with such startling clarity that in a photograph it is often difficult to decide which is the right way up. An hour-and-a-quarter's walk farther up this tumble of ridges is Lake Gault, haunt of the comparatively rare crested grebe, a shag-like bird with two pen-like quills protruding from its head; and, in the lake's surrounding bush, the *kaka* (native bush parrot). The view from Lake Gault is even finer than that from Lake Matheson, a wide panorama of peaks, from the Fritz Range on the left with the névé of its glacier, through Silberhorn and Teichelmann to the stepped peak of Mount Cook on the far right.

The road running over the ridges goes through native forest of exceptional beauty, down to Gillespies Beach, once a gold-rush settlement extracting gold from the sands of the beach, a process known as "black-sanding". It is difficult, and perhaps impossible, to obtain a reliable estimate of how many people lived in this settlement in its heyday, but it is known that they were sufficient to support several pubs and the odd dancehall. The settlement, when it died in 1910, had grown to include eleven shops, two butcheries, two bakeries, a school, a chapel and one hotel. The chapel was razed in 1933, when a big bucket dredge started to operate and needed to go through the site. In 1946, the gold seemed to have run out, and there is now little to be seen of the old township. But two brothers named Shaw moved in some years ago, built a homestead and began to farm. They turned their hands, also, to black-sanding the beach for gold, an activity which is beginning to increase hereabouts – a

sort of gold-rush renaissance. Farther down the beach, north of the settlement site, is a seal colony. The seals are fairly approachable, though the old bulls will usually put on a display, bellowing and gnashing their tusks, and it is exceedingly dangerous to get between them and the sea.

Franz Josef Glacier

The stretch of road which leaves Fox Glacier and heads north is the most tortuous stretch of highway on the West Coast, and possibly the most twisty piece of road in New Zealand. It undulates over the toes of the mountains, snaking around steep faces, turning back upon itself, clinging to the faces of bluffs and running beneath steep hillsides to which the bush clings precariously. Most of these ridges are ancient glacial moraines, a fact which becomes apparent in some of the road cuttings, which reveal unstable conglomerate packed between ice-scratched boulders.

The road runs out of the Omoeroa Range and into the broad Waiho valley, with Canavans Knob rising off to the left, so isolated as to be unmistakable, a dome of granite shaped and polished by the ice-age glaciers, and forest marching away from its base, containing all of the lowland types of indigenous pine.

The road crosses the Waiho river, whose name means "Smoky

Above: The Franz Josef glacier is shorter than the Fox, flowing 12 kilometres
(7½ miles) down a rather steeper valley
Opposite: Lake Matheson, its still waters reflecting the mountains and forest
around it, developed out of "dead" ice left behind by the Fox Glacier

Waters", which some believe may refer to the milky appearance due to
the rock flour held in suspension in its waters, and others say refers to the
vapour rising continually from the ice-cold water. Just across the river is
Franz Josef village, built on the northern slope of an ancient moraine. On
the left, where the road enters the village, is the delightful little Anglican
Church of St James, surrounded by well-kept lawn and shaded by native
trees. It is famous chiefly for the window over its altar, through which,
when it was first built, the Franz Josef Glacier could be seen descending
into forest of almost tropical luxuriance. Now the glacier has receded too
far to afford such a view, but the window still surmounts the altar with a
picturesque view of the Fritz Range's snow-covered peaks rising above the
darkly bush-draped hills, more beautiful and more appropriate in this
place than any stained glass saints.

The Franz Josef Glacier was named by the geologist, Sir Julius von
Haast, after the Emperor of Austria. Actually, he named it Francis
Joseph, out of deference to the English origins of his Canterbury country-
men. But various forms of the name kept appearing on subsequent maps
and geographies, and the earliest official form on Lands and Survey
Department maps and in the Year Book was Franz Joseph. Eventually and
happily the name reverted to its purely Austrian form.

The Maoris called it Ka Roimata-o-Hine-Hukatere, a beautiful name

Ribbons of water flowing off the Franz Josef Glacier, named after the Austro-Hungarian emperor

which means "Tears of the Avalanche Girl". She shed them, according to legend, over a man named Wawe, a confirmed plainsman who feared and mistrusted her beloved mountains but strove, for love of her, to overcome his fears and adapt himself to life amongst the high peaks. He inevitably slipped and fell to his death, and her tears of remorse flowed down the valley until the old gods, out of pity, turned them into a river of ice, a memorial to Wawe.

The approach road, like that into Fox Glacier, runs for a considerable distance through forest, but undulates rather more. The glacier comes into view quite suddenly, the whole gleaming length of it from its névé high in the mountains between the Baird and Fritz Ranges to its terminal face, no longer quite so spectacular as that of the Fox. Indeed, it seems to dribble off to a spaced spread of smallish ice blocks on top of the terminal moraine, though a closer inspection will reveal that there is still a massive depth of ice there. It has pushed ahead of it a bigger rock pile than that which faces the Fox, and the rocks now form a protective wall across its face. The Waiho, rushing away from the glacier, carries with it great chunks of ice broken from the even bigger chunks which, too big to float in the comparatively shallow waters, lie on the bed until the turbulent stream smashes them into small pieces and tumbles them away downstream. It is a swifter river than the Fox.

In the vicinity is a fault-line, a cyclopean split in the old earth's crust, formed, so geologists say, by one side of the South Island moving, luckily with infinite slowness, and the other side remaining stationary. The

Lovely Lake Mapourika, near the Franz Josef Glacier, offers visitors trout fishing, boating and swimming as well as occasional glimpses of the rare white heron

fracture is undoubtedly deep, for now and again you catch a whiff of sulphur, and there are hot springs in the area.

The valley is magnificent, all steep slopes and rock walls, with waterfalls leaping down through great rifts in the rugged faces, ducking beneath boulders wedged in crevices, or leaping off them as though they were springboards.

As at Fox Glacier, there are fascinating walks, to such places as Peter's Pool, which provides a perfect example of how nature regenerates the forest which was destroyed by the glacier's advances in times past. The pool was a piece of "dead" ice, which melted and formed a deep pool, into which the surrounding gravels began to crumble. This stage was reached around 1800. Before long, earth washed into the pool and, with the gravels, provided nourishment for underwater plant life; and soon reedy plants began to emerge from the shallow waters at the pool's edge. Waterborne vegetation decayed, laying down peat, making the pool shallower, and the reedy growth at the edge rotted down and provided a foothold for more growth, so that the pool is diminishing in depth and area. Eventually the pool will cease to exist. Grasses will grow over it, sheltering shrub seedlings, which, as they develop, will in turn shelter timber-tree seedlings; and at some time in the future, the area devastated by the advance of the glacier will be forested over.

The bush in the vicinity of these glaciers is positively primeval, including plants such as *Tmesipteris tannensis*, whose ancestors flourished on earth 160 million years before the first dinosaurs.

Above: The historic old wharf at Okarito, South Westland, to which coastal
shipping once came to serve the gold-mining towns of the region
Opposite: The white heron, called *kotuku* by the Maori, has only one breeding place
in New Zealand (Okarito), but is occasionally seen in other parts of the country

---

The whole countryside is built on a stupendous scale, with forests, the
wild streams like the Waiho and the Callery rivers, which latter fights its
way impatiently and awesomely through the narrow fissure known as
Callery Gorge, and the Warm Springs, which spill over into the frigid
Waiho river, sending up clouds of steam. It is a gigantic juxtaposition of
forest of almost tropical luxuriance, thermal activity and the Franz Josef
Glacier with, over all, the brooding Alps. And there is the strange,
brilliant light which shines out of the glacier valleys, especially noticeable
on grey days, telling you where they are before you come in sight of them.

The South Westland Lakes

Eight kilometres (five miles) of winding road north of Franz Josef is Lake
Mapourika, largest of the South Westland lakes, 11 square kilometres (7
square miles) in area and about 37m (120ft) deep at its deepest part. Yet
another ice-remnant from a prehistoric glacier, Mapourika is a peaceful,
forest-fringed water whose name was not, as it happens, bestowed by the
Maoris, but by the *Pakeha*, being the name of a ship which maintained a
direct service between Westland and Australia in the goldrush days.

It is typical of the lakes in this region, which include the somewhat
smaller wilderness lagoon, Okarito, where, in that long, boisterous era
between 1868 and 1907, some 5000 miners worked and patronised the
hotels, casinos, dance halls, banks and shops which, hardly believable
today, spread along the edge of Okarito Lagoon. Now it is the nesting
place for *kotuku*, the beautiful white heron, strictly protected.

Across the Waitangi-taona river, where it spreads out across the flat

from the feet of the Price Range, gravel from its winter floods has spread over the floor of the forest, choking out the undergrowth and also gradually killing the *kahikatea* trees. The river brings down such enormous quantities of gravel from the mountains that its bed rises about 30cm (12 inches) each year.

The small township of Whataroa lies along this road, a self-sufficient little community sitting amid bush-patched fields. From the Whataroa valley the way goes over Mount Hercules, through the Saltwater State Forest, a scenic reserve area signposted with rough-hewn planks of wood indicating the boundaries of the reserve. On the mountain's northern side, the road goes down to the Poerua river and across the flatland it shares with the Wanganui (another one), a spread of farmland backed by high mountains and occupied by the tiny settlement of Harihari. The Poerua valley is noted for fine dairy cattle, claimed to be the most productive in Westland.

North of Harihari, Lake Ianthe Scenic Reserve contains, as well as Lake Ianthe, a giant *matai* tree with a bole some 5.3m (17ft) in diameter, estimated to be over 1000 years old. The lake is famed as a trout-fishing water – all South Westland lakes are, but Lake Ianthe especially so – where both brown and rainbow trout abound.

People visit shimmering, bush-fringed Lake Kaniere, east of Hokitika, for the beauty of its setting and the superb boating and fishing available on its quiet waters

Lake Ianthe was named by a surveyor-explorer who admired Byron's poetry. Byron's *Childe Harold's Pilgrimage* was dedicated to a little girl named Ianthe, which makes the naming of the lake a sort of oblique compliment to Byron. Anyway, it is a pretty name for a pretty water.

The next town to the north is Ross, once a goldrush town with a population of about 2800, now a village with only about a tenth of that number. In 1903, in adjacent diggings was found the largest nugget ever won in New Zealand, a solid 99 ounces troyweight. It was raffled to raise funds for a local hospital, and was won by a publican in Hokitika, who actually used it as a door stopper. Subsequently it was given to King George V as a gesture of loyalty.

Hokitika was once the largest of the goldrush towns, and still looks not unlike one, with its little wood and corrugated iron shops lining a narrow street, and a prodigiously wide main street running away from it, wide enough to accommodate goodness knows how many bullock teams abreast. If its streets, in its heyday, were not actually paved with gold, at least it can be said that, like the Irishman's London in the old song, *Mountains of Mourne*, there were "people all working by day and by night", with "gangs of them digging for gold in the street" – and that's more than Dick Whittington's London could boast, for all that irrepressible urchin's expectations. Today Hokitika is a somewhat somnolent little country town, a sawmilling and farming centre, though still the town which, of all Westland towns, epitomises the "West Coaster".

For West Coasters are almost an ethnic entity. Your true Coaster is a warm person, more than ordinarily hospitable. Descendant of the old gold-seekers, he still speaks with a faint remnant of the Australian drawl, and with the Australian's frequently highly original turn of phrase. His warmth and hospitality are frequently masked by a suggestion of cynicism, an apparently sardonic view of and commentary on his world.

There is a small museum in Hokitika, mainly concerned with the gold-seeking days, but also possessing some fine Maori artifacts. But the real *pièce de resistance*, the one which says the most about those wild days when fortunes were hard sought and easily lost, is the lockup, containing one fiendishly uncomfortable iron bed – even the mattress base consists of strips of iron of a hefty gauge – and men's and women's leg-irons, various gyves and fetters, and a no-nonsense barred cell door that would defy a light tank.

Eastwards from Hokitika is Lake Kaniere, a forest-fringed jewel of a lake, a holiday resort for Greymouth and Hokitika people, who have built a small vacation village on its shore. The lake itself is wide and deep, a greatly favoured boating water.

Between Hokitika and Greymouth, the road keeps to the flat coastal shelf, except for a few kilometres between Kumara and a locality called Camerons, where it runs over some coastward-trending spurs and crosses the Taramakau river. At Kumara, a road turns inland, climbing upward and eastward, through the village of Otira with its long, rusty locomotive sheds and tiny houses. The sheds house the electric locomotives which haul trains through New Zealand's longest railway tunnel, 9 kilometres (5½ miles) long, cut through the Southern Alps. The road crosses over the Otira river and starts up the Otira Gorge, where the vegetation begins to change from rain forest to mountain beech forest, with a good sprinkling of *rata*. The lovely little Reed's Falls flow out beneath the road just before it swings across Candy's Creek, where there is a fearsome scree

The Upper Otira valley in Arthur's Pass National Park which spreads over both sides of the Main Divide of the Southern Alps to offer great scenic contrasts

slide poised above the road, which loops around Candy's Bend, from where, at the rest area, a splendid view is obtained of the gorge, revealed here as a dark and twisting gash in the ranges, where a surly stream bullies its way past the boulders and beneath the drab and dripping bush. It is a very beautiful scene, a little awesome, which was painted in a brooding picture by the Dutch-New Zealand artist, Petrus van der Velden, in 1912.

Arthur's Pass township, on the eastern side of the Main Divide, is headquarters for climbers, skiers and people who just happen to love a mountain holiday. Its waterfalls, walks and forest scenery are unexcelled.

North from the Otira turnoff is Greymouth, Westland's largest town, with a population of about 11,500. Sandwiched between the steep, forested hills and the Erua Moana and Kororo lagoons, it is an attractive town, which reaches back into the valleys between the bush-clad spurs of the ranges. Beside it, the Grey river flows strongly and swiftly out to sea, and in the hills around it are old mining settlements like Marsden and Rutherglen, and the little forest lakes, Haupiri and Hochstetter. When the gold ran out, many of the old goldminers stayed to mine the vast coal reserves in this part of the country, and Greymouth could be said to have a foot in both camps, with goldmining settlements to the south of the

Rock stacks formed by wind and erosion stand off the Westland coast north of Greymouth

Shantytown, at Rutherglen south of Greymouth, is a reconstruction of a typical West Coast gold-mining town complete with bank, hotel, stores and stables

town, and coalmines near at hand and to the north. The demarkation is more one of time than of space, and much gold was won north of Greymouth; but whereas the transition in the south has been from gold to farming, to the north and in Greymouth's vicinity it has been more markedly from gold to coal. Greymouth reflects neither of these activities, particularly. It has the appearance of a planned town rather than a haphazard mesh of streets.

Near Rutherglen, a few kilometres to the south of Greymouth, is Shantytown. A creation of the 1960s, it is nevertheless a typical goldrush town, its buildings mostly genuine goldrush buildings, brought together from several localities, and built to resemble the original mining town of Rutherglen as it was in the '60s and '70s of last century. A description of old-time Rutherglen is a description of Shantytown. *The Grey River Argus*, in 1867, described Rutherglen thus:

"My first impression on entering the township was one of surprise at the really fine spacious stores and hotels, and the air of active business which pervaded the place . . . The street of Rutherglen is about a couple of hundred yards in length; having a good fall, it is free from the mud and waterholes which are generally pervading characteristics of a diggings-town street."

And that, really, is the impression one receives of Shantytown. Its railway station is a perfect replica, built from New Zealand Railways plans, and serving a train which a restored Kaitangata-class locomotive hauls on a nostalgic, coal-smoky, hissing and clanking run through the bush. Its stables shelter a genuine Cobb & Co. coach, which takes passengers over a bush road, fording Infants Creek and passing through old gold claims. There are shops whose shelves carry labels long forgotten, and even a Chinese den, an Orientally secretive place close to that indispensable public utility, the genuine two-holer dunny.

There is a hospital also, a bright, clean, cheerful place, a spell in which, after months in some rough shanty, must have seemed a holiday.

"Camerons Livery and Bait Stables", brought from a West Coast gold-mining locality and faithfully reconstructed at Shantytown

North from Greymouth, the coast road passes through Punakaiki, where a warm current sweeps close inshore, creating a magnificent beach and, with the sheltering curve of the Paparoa Range, a micro-climate which is almost sub-tropical so that *nikau* palms nod and sway along the coast, and luxuriant rain forest clothes the flanks of the mountains. The Paparoa Range rises up at its highest point, Mount Uriah, to a mere 1500m (4291ft) above sea level, low enough to allow the moisture-laden clouds from the Tasman Sea to pass over and drop their burden of rain over the higher country around the St Arnaud and Spenser mountains. Punakaiki, therefore, gets a more generous share of sunshine that do the regions to the south along this coast.

There are interesting rock formations here known as Pancake Rocks. Reaching into the sea off Dolomite Point, the rocks are well if obviously named. They really do look like stacks of enormous pancakes, an effect created by the action of wind and sea on a limestone headland. In this vicinity are the Putai Blowholes and the Paku Surge Pool, created by the sea's eroding of chambers in the rocks. The explosive effect of air trapped in the caverns by incoming surges has created blowholes. The water-spouts, performed to the accompaniment of rumblings and boomings deep underfoot, are best observed at high tide, when there is a good sea running.

Punakaiki is not, as it happens, in Westland, being just over the provincial boundary in Nelson province. The road runs northward, around cliffs from which breathtaking seascapes are seen, and dipping and climbing through delightful native forest. It passes through Charleston, once a lusty mining town with eighty pubs, dancehalls and gambling helldorados and all the usual trimmings, with plenty of Australian dancehall girls, landed on the nearby coast and carried ashore on the shoulders of husky miners. Today they are all gone, and the grandilo-quently-named Nile river, along which the goldseekers toiled, is once again a brawling little creek, frequented mainly by weekend amateur

The famous "Pancake Rocks" at Punakaiki are stratified limestone rocks where,
in heavy weather, the displays of blown spray are spectacular

panners, seeking gold as a mere hobby. One goldmine still operates as a commercial proposition, but one suspects that its owner and his wife, receive at least as much from tourists as they do from gold recovered.

Between Charleston and Westport, much of the land is *pakihi* country, where a hard claypan has interfered with natural drainage, with the result that the rather desolate landscape between Cape Foulwind (named by Cook) and the inland ranges is patched with swamp and coarse scrub.

Westport is to coalmining what Hokitika was to goldmining. The towns are similar, four-square little communities sitting right on the windswept coast, though Westport is somewhat bigger than Hokitika. It possesses a unique museum, the Coaltown Museum, where visitors may enter a most life-like replica of a coalmine, crunching over coal, seeing the blackened walls and props of rough timber dimly in wide-spaced lights, and hearing some little distance off the voices and picks of miners, and the dripping of water – no place for the claustrophobic.

From Westport, the way goes north, through small coalmining settlements, such as Millerton, near which is the Burning Mine, extending over an area of some 81ha (200 acres), where there is an estimated 15-million tonnes of coal. For 70 years, efforts have been made to extinguish the fire, but the holocaust continues unabated, melting the sandstone rocks into strange and fanciful shapes.

The coast road climbs over Karamea Bluff and descends to Little Wanganui, a sort of winterless fairyland of green fields, where donkeys and peacocks may be seen in the paddocks, and the Little Wanganui river meanders peaceably across the flat and spills into the Karamea Bight.

Karamea, a hamlet with a population of about 300, has a fine little museum, and limestone caves in which, a few years ago, a complete *moa* skeleton was found.

The road ends at Kohaihai Bluffs, some 16 kilometres (10 miles) north of Karamea, and the next reachable village is Collingwood on Golden Bay, which is at the northern end of the Heaphy Track, an extremely popular four-day walk which begins along the coast, past beautiful white-sand beaches, follows the Heaphy river inland, wanders over open tops with views of forest-filled river valleys, over the Gouland Downs and across the Perry Saddle to Brown Hut on the Brown river, 25 kilometres (15 miles) by road from Collingwood.

There is another way out of Westport, going eastward through the Buller Gorge, a great, rock-walled, powerful river gorge, to Inangahua Junction, from which a road runs south to Reefton, thence over the Rahu Saddle, through Springs Junction and Maruia Springs thermal springs resort, and over the Lewis Pass to Canterbury.

Another road goes north from Inangahua Junction, following the Buller river through forest-filled, bluff-browed gorges to Nelson Lakes National Park, 57,256ha (over 114,000 acres) of country as crumpled as a carelessly dropped rug, product of prehistoric glaciation and continual block-faulting, walled on its eastern side by the St Arnaud and Travers ranges. The lakes which give the park its name are Rotoroa ("Long Lake") and Rotoiti ("Small Lake"), lying in valleys scooped out by Ice Age glaciers. Lake Rotoiti's valley was formed by a glacier which slipped down from the Travers Saddle, gouging out a considerable trench beneath the St Arnaud Range and Robert Ridge, the northern extremity of the Travers Range. The glacier came up against a block of black basalt, spewed up by a volcano when this land was a flat and featureless seabed,

Badlands on the Heaphy Track, the superb four-to-six day walk between Golden Bay and the West Coast on the northern tip of the South Island

The beech forest-surrounded glacial Lake Rotoroa is one of two lakes at the heart of the Nelson Lakes National Park

and had to fork around either side of this massive obstruction, known today as Black Hill. There it stopped, ultimately to melt; and snow-melt from the surrounding mountains swelled the streams and filled the valley until it spilled over and flowed out down the long, twisting valley, to become the Buller river.

Rotoroa, also, was an ancient glacier, 15 kilometres (9½ miles) long as compared with Rotoiti's 8 kilometres (9 miles). It lies at an altitude nearly 150m (492ft) lower than Rotoiti's 610m (2000ft). It is deeper than Rotoiti – 145m at its deepest point.

The mountains surrounding Rotoroa are low enough to be bush-clad right over their tops. The St Arnaud Range, towering above Lake Rotoiti and dipping its forested spurs into the lake, is snow-capped for much of the year. Both lakes are forested to their very brink. The countryside around them is laced with walks, from short strolls about the village of St Arnaud to days-long hikes over mountain passes, through the high beech forests and around small lakes and tarns. Both lakes are favoured for pleasure-boating, and both are excellent trout waters. On the northern end of Robert Ridge, on the 1411m (4630ft) Mount Robert, there are ski huts and some good skiing slopes.

North, over Golden Downs, through the huge, man-made Golden Downs State Forest, the road runs, down through Wakefield, that small, attractive town on the south-western edge of the Waimea Plain, through Richmond and Stoke, to Nelson.

Index

Figures in italics refer to illustration captions

Photographic Acknowledgements

J. Allan Cash Photolibrary, London, England, pages 101, 105 bottom, 120, 142–143, 144, 151, 174, 175, 177, 181, 184, 196; Bay Picture Library, Sydney, Australia, pages 51, 103, 141, 194, 240, 244; Bruce Coleman Ltd., London, England, pages 10, 112–113, 128–129; Greg Evans Photo Library, London, England, pages 40–41, 82, 148–149, 245; Ronald Ivan Israel, London, England, pages 43, 68, 200, 237, 238; Photobank Image Library, Auckland, New Zealand, title-spread, pages 6–7, 9, 17, 22, 24–25, 45, 48, 53, 54, 55, 56, 59, 60–61, 62, 66, 71, 73, 76–77, 80–81, 83, 85, 87, 88–89, 93, 100, 108–109, 111, 116, 117, 121, 126, 127, 132–133, 134, 135, 136, 146, 162, 168–169, 176, 180, 184–185, 188, 198, 206–207, 208, 218–219, 220–221, 222, 227, 242–243, 250; Photographic Library of Australia, Sydney, Australia, pages 8, 12–13, 18, 19, 20–21, 28–29, 33, 34, 36, 37, 38–39, 44, 57, 58, 63, 64–65, 67, 75, 79, 84, 86, 91, 92, 94, 95, 102, 106–107, 110, 123, 130, 137, 138, 140, 145, 150, 156, 158, 159, 160, 161, 170–171, 172–173, 178, 179, 182, 186–187, 188–189, 192, 193, 194–195, 197, 199, 201, 202–203, 209, 210, 211, 213, 214–215, 228–229, 230, 236, 239, 241, 246, 251; The Photo Source/CLI, London, England, pages 69, 154–155, 183; G.R. Roberts, Nelson, New Zealand, pages 16, 30, 46–47, 50, 74, 78, 90, 96–97, 105 top, 115, 118, 122, 124, 153, 157, 166–167, 169, 190–191, 205, 216, 217, 222–223, 224–225, 231, 232, 233, 244–245, 248–249; Spectrum Colour Library, London, England, pages 12, 26, 29, 204, 212; Judy Todd, London, England, pages 11, 14–15, 27, 99, 114, 152, 154, 163, 165, 218, 234

Front cover: Lake Te Anau, South Island (Robert van de Voort, Profimage, Auckland, New Zealand)
Back cover: General Store and Pier, Opua, North Island (Spectrum Colour Library, London, England)
Titlespread: Lake Te Anau, South Island (Photobank Image Library, Auckland, New Zealand)